A Reference Publication in Literature
Ronald Gottesman, *Editor*

James Weldon Johnson and
Arna Wendell Bontemps:
A Reference Guide

Robert E. Fleming

G. K. HALL & CO., 70 LINCOLN STREET, BOSTON, MASS.

Copyright © 1978 by Robert E. Fleming

Library of Congress Cataloging in Publication Data

Fleming, Robert E
    James Weldon Johnson and Arna Wendell Bontemps.

    (A reference publication in literature)
    Includes index.
    1. Johnson, James Weldon, 1871-1938--Bibliography.
2. Bontemps, Arna Wendell, 1902-1973--Bibliography.
I. Title. II. Series: Reference publications in
literature.
Z8455.65.F58 [PS3519.O2625]   016.818'5'209   77-23874
  ISBN 0-8161-7932-8

This publication is printed on permanent/durable acid-free paper
MANUFACTURED IN THE UNITED STATES OF AMERICA

Contents

Preface

I have attempted to see all books and periodicals in English that discuss the two authors and have listed and annotated all the items I have seen unless the writers were merely mentioned or the materials were simply brief introductions in anthologies. For items that I was not able to see because the periodical or book was not available, my source for the entry is given. For items that were not located in the place cited, the notation "unlocatable" is employed, and the source of the entry is noted.

Because entries are arranged according to the year of publication, a reader can follow not only the writer's creative progress but also changes in the critical reception of his works. To convey the attitude of the various critics and reviewers I have sometimes quoted significant phrases within my annotations. In addition, I have always employed the terms the original critic uses for the race of the author—negro, Negro, colored, Afro-American, black, or Black—since this may indicate something of the tone of the review or essay. Early writers such as Charles W. Chesnutt fought hard to have their race termed "Negro" rather than "negro," since the capitalization of the term suggested increased respect. The term "colored" may be complimentary or derogatory depending on its historical setting; the National Association for the Advancement of Colored People (N.A.A.C.P.) was founded at a time when "colored" was a respectable term for the Afro-American, but in a modern setting the term would be regarded as insulting. Finally, in recent years it has frequently been a mark of self-respect to capitalize the word "Black."

Each index lists the titles of all books and articles that are devoted chiefly to Johnson or Bontemps as well as the authors of all books, articles, and reviews. Under the titles of the book length works by these two authors, all discussions of those works are listed—reviews as well as longer pieces. In addition, under the heading of the author himself are sub-topics such as "awards and honors," "letters," and "biography."

I wish to thank Keitha Shoupe of the Interlibrary Loan division, Zimmerman Library, University of New Mexico, for her patience and

Preface

industry in ordering materials, and I wish to thank my wife Esther for her advice and her help in preparing the manuscript. Finally, my thanks to Grace Nail Johnson for the encouragement she has given me in my various studies of her late husband's work.

James Weldon Johnson

Introduction

Considering the times in which he lived and worked, an outline of the life of James Weldon Johnson sounds like the plot for a Horatio Alger novel. Born on June 17, 1871, in Jacksonville, Florida, by no means the most prejudiced city in the South, Johnson nevertheless could not attend high school in his home town because schools were segregated and public education was not provided for black students after the eighth grade. He therefore attended the preparatory school division of Atlanta University, from which he later took his bachelor's degree.

Back in Jacksonville after his graduation, Johnson began to establish the pattern of outstanding achievements that would mark his later life. Over a period of eight years, Johnson served as principal and teacher at Stanton, his old grammar school, where he added high school instruction to the curriculum. While working at this full time job, he founded a black newspaper, the Daily American, and served as its editor, attacking racial injustice and offering advice to black readers. After the financial collapse of this enterprise he studied law and was admitted to the Florida bar in spite of a hostile examining board. Meanwhile Johnson continued to write poetry, an avocation since his years at Atlanta, publishing his dialect poem "Sence You Went Away" in the prestigious Century Magazine and collaborating with his brother J. Rosamond Johnson on the writing of "Lift Every Voice and Sing," a song that would eventually be known as the "Negro National Anthem."

Leaving Jacksonville in 1902, Johnson joined his brother in New York City and the two, in partnership with Bob Cole, embarked on a brief but impressive career writing songs and musical comedy. During the same period Johnson found the time to attend Professor Brander Matthews' classes at Columbia University and to involve himself in Republican politics, an activity which led to the next phase of his career, as U.S. Consul to Puerto Cabello, Venezuela and Corinto, Nicaragua, from 1906 to 1912 under the Roosevelt administration. In Latin America Johnson continued to work at his writing, producing poems and a novel.

INTRODUCTION — JAMES WELDON JOHNSON

On leaving the diplomatic service, Johnson became an editorial writer for The New York Age, an influential black newspaper, from which he moved to a position with the National Association for the Advancement of Colored People, first serving as a field worker, organizing new branches and investigating racial incidents. In 1920 he was elected Secretary of the N.A.A.C.P., the first black man to hold that powerful post. During his tenure, Johnson lobbied vigorously for a federal anti-lynching bill, fought a major battle over the staffing of a hospital for black veterans, and increased both the membership and the effectiveness of the organization. Moreover, he continued to carry out writing and editing projects. In 1930, however, he returned to the career that he had entered after graduation from college, accepting a chair in creative writing at Fisk University, a post that he held until his death in an auto accident on June 26, 1938.

Like his life, Johnson's writing shows an astonishing versatility rather than concentrated mastery of any single field. Beginning as a rather conventional poet, Johnson went on to write popular songs, a highly influential novel, experimental verse, informal history, an autobiography, a polemical book, and numerous articles; through his critical articles and the prefaces to three significant anthologies, he became one of the leading critical voices of his day in the field of black American literature.

Johnson's 1917 collection Fifty Years and Other Poems, a sampling of his best work from the previous twenty years, suggests his struggle to define both his subject matter and the form he would use to convey it. The contents range from non-racial poetry in the Anglo-American tradition stressed in his literary education to dialect verse familiar to readers of Paul Laurence Dunbar. That Johnson had solved his problem of a fitting idiom for racial poetry was evident in 1927 with the publication of God's Trombones, in which he deliberately rejected dialect as "a quite limited instrument" capable only of portraying a comic "happy-go-lucky" type of stage Negro or of presenting a pathetic "forlorn figure."[1] Johnson, who had come to New York during the heyday of the "coon song" and had written somewhat genteel songs within that genre, wanted to leave its taint behind when he set out to create serious and moving poetry. Consequently, he attempted to capture the uniqueness of the black preacher's idiom by employing some of his eccentricities of vocabulary and the rhythms of his speech while avoiding "the mere mutilation of English spelling and pronunciation."[2] Johnson's compromise between dialect and standard literary English was successful in retaining the flavor of black speech while at the same time emphasizing the dignity of the black orator, and for the most part his efforts were well received.

Johnson's career as a novelist was less extensive than his involvement with poetry but was just as significant. During his years in New York Johnson began a novel about the search for identity of a man who is light enough to pass for white but who admires his mother's

race and wants to be "a great colored man." While at his post in
Venezuela, Johnson finished this novel, which was published anony-
mously in 1912. A work of art as well as a social document, The
Autobiography of an Ex-Colored Man is an important novel. Johnson's
depiction of a light-skinned black man is profound in its psychological insights and is executed with consummate literary skill, so that
the novel may be read on more than one level. Indeed, because the
protagonist lives in both North and South, in rural America and cit-
ies, and even in Europe, and because he frequently stops the action
of the novel to comment on racial attitudes, the novel has often been
cited as an exposé and criticism of American racism. Both the psychological and social facets of the book influenced black writers
after Johnson, from the novelists of the twenties who also treat
"passing"--Walter White, Nella Larsen, and Jessie Fauset--to later
naturalists who examine social conditions--Richard Wright and Chester
Himes--and to novelists who couple social criticism with psychological
probing--most notably Ralph Ellison.

Johnson also distinguished himself as a writer of history with
Black Manhattan (1930), to which other historians remain indebted,
and as the author of an autobiography, Along This Way (1933), which
has been praised as an informal history of his times since Johnson
played a part in so many of the literary, social, and political move-
ments of his day. As a critic and a compiler of early anthologies of
black poetry and music, Johnson defended the artistic achievements of
his race and explained their origins and meaning to a white world
which was incredibly naive about black America.

On the whole, Johnson fared better with the critics than many
other black American writers. The reception of his first two books,
The Autobiography of an Ex-Colored Man (1912) and Fifty Years and
Other Poems (1917), was generally polite if limited. Most reviewers
approached the fictional autobiography either as a genuine autobiography or as a vehicle for commentary on American race relations, there-
by establishing a critical trend that would last for some fifty years,
in spite of a few perceptive critics who felt that the novel had real
depth as a work of art.

The earliest of these sympathetic critics was Brander Matthews,
the Columbia University English professor whose classes Johnson had
attended during his New York years. Matthews paid the novel the compliment of discussing it in company with William Dean Howells' New
Leaf Mills and Robert Herrick's One Woman's Life in his essay-review
for Munsey's Magazine (1913.B2). He asserted that the key to a book's
longevity was the strength of its characters and its author's refusal
to depend too heavily on plot. His view of Autobiography as a novel
of character contradicted that of most other reviewers: that the plot
was the remarkable feature of the novel and that its main value for
white readers was the insight it offered into the life of black people.
Matthews, who had talked with Johnson about problems the latter faced
in .writing the novel, of course had advantages in getting to the heart
of the work.

Introduction — James Weldon Johnson

Critics of both races responded favorably to Fifty Years and
Other Poems. Reviewing the volume for the Boston Evening Transcript
(1917.B1), the conservative black critic William Stanley Braithwaite
made the obvious comparison between the current poems and those of
the recently deceased Paul Laurence Dunbar, and, surprisingly, pre-
ferred Johnson's poetry because of the poet's deeper intellect and
his freedom from Dunbar's "sensuality." Like Braithwaite, Benjamin
Brawley, who reviewed the book for The Journal of Negro History
(1918.B5), stated that Johnson had established himself as one of the
leading poets of his race. Brander Matthews wrote in his introduction
to the book (1917.B2) that Johnson had shown the ability to write in
both of the earlier veins of black poetry--serious verse indistinguishable from that of white poets and verse on racial themes written
in dialect--but had also experimented with serious racial themes expressed in the best poetic form. Works such as the title poem, which
commemorated the Emancipation, represented this promising mode, Matthews felt.

In spite of a few favorable reviews, Johnson's reputation as a
writer began to grow only in the 1920's, undoubtedly aided by his new
prominence as Secretary of the N.A.A.C.P. and the growing interest of
literary people such as Eugene O'Neill, Sherwood Anderson, and Carl
Van Vechten in Afro-American culture and art, an interest that would
give rise to the Harlem Renaissance. Johnson's three anthologies,
The Book of American Negro Poetry (1922), The Book of American Negro
Spirituals (1925), and The Second Book of American Negro Spirituals
(1926), were all widely reviewed not only in such black publications
as The Journal of Negro History, Opportunity, and The Crisis, but
also in such prestigious journals of the white literary establishment
as The Bookman, The Nation, The New Republic, The Dial, and The Saturday Review of Literature. While some reviewers expressed reservations
about certain poems in the first of these volumes, none found serious
fault with Johnson's introductions to the three collections. Reviewers included critics who were friends of Johnson (Walter White, Mary
White Ovington, and Carl Van Vechten, for example); however, such
eminent literary figures as H. L. Mencken and Mark Van Doren joined
them in praising Johnson's efforts as an anthologist and critic.

Johnson's career as a creative writer gained a new and wider recognition in 1927 with the publication of a second volume of his own verse,
God's Trombones. Although some critics looked upon this book more as
folklore than as art, most reviewers realized that Johnson's strategy
for capturing the idiom of the black rural preacher without using dialect was an original and praiseworthy experiment, and Harriet Monroe
of Poetry magazine felt that readers "should be grateful for the book"
(1927.B21). Knopf's reprinting of The Autobiography of an Ex-Colored
Man,[3] this time with Johnson identified as the author, brought the
novel a much larger, and in some cases a more perceptive, audience than
did its first publication; the anonymous reviewer for the Times Literary Supplement (1928.B4) noted that the novel contained psychological
complexity as well as social commentary.

Introduction — James Weldon Johnson

By the end of the decade, Johnson was well established as a literary figure. When he turned to history with the publication of Black Manhattan (1930), Johnson met an enthusiastic response from nearly every reviewer of the book. Only an anonymous critic for Spectator (1930.B9) had any serious reservations, and he objected on the moral grounds that the book tended to emphasize "unworthy heroes" such as athletes and entertainers rather than more intellectual figures. Overall, if Johnson had anticipated the Harlem Renaissance with The Autobiography and Fifty Years and helped to usher it in with his edition of The Book of American Negro Poetry, he emerged from it with one of the most secure literary reputations among writers of his race. Even if his health had not dictated retirement from the stress-filled N.A.A.C.P. post, Johnson might have felt justified in resigning to pursue his literary interests, especially since an attractive teaching post at Fisk University offered him a degree of financial security.

The first half of the 1930's was a productive period for Johnson. His revised edition of The Book of American Negro Poetry came out in 1931 and was deemed even better than his first noteworthy anthology. His autobiography Along This Way (1933) was praised not only as an unusual success story but as proof that black people could survive the indignities and dangers of American life without becoming embittered about race. Even Johnson's polemical book Negro Americans, What Now? (1934) attracted a number of favorable reviews by white critics although Johnson's old colleague W. E. B. DuBois complained in his review for the New York Herald Tribune (1934.B9) that the book was too meek and old-fashioned, and that it displayed Johnson's ignorance of modern economics. The last of his books to be published before Johnson's death, Saint Peter Relates an Incident: Selected Poems (1935) was generally regarded as disappointing in comparison with God's Trombones; however, William Rose Benét praised it in The Saturday Review of Literature (1936.B1), calling Johnson "one of the best" black poets.

Johnson's sudden death in an auto accident in 1938 stimulated a flurry of complimentary obituaries and eulogies. Old enmities were forgotten as both races paid tribute to Johnson as a writer, a political leader, and a man. A special issue of The Crisis was made up, consisting of tributes from notable officials of the N.A.A.C.P., a statement by Mayor Fiorello LaGuardia, sonnets in praise of the fallen leader, and excerpts from over fifty obituaries which had appeared in newspapers across the nation. Only black historian Kelly Miller sounded a note of opposition in his column in The New York Age (1938.B18). Calling Johnson the "Negro Poet Laureate," Miller charged that he had been a "literary dilettante" whose reputation was based on his never giving offense to the white race, rather than on any great ability as a poet. Few agreed with this view, however, and Johnson's final position was that of a mourned elder statesman in politics and literature. The following year a tasteful memorial brochure was issued by Fisk University, collecting the reminiscences of Arthur Spingarn, Carl Van Vechten, and the respected black literary critic Sterling A. Brown.

Introduction — James Weldon Johnson

In spite of his popularity during the 1920's and 1930's Johnson
was almost forgotten as a writer during the twenty years that followed
his death. Only an occasional article in Opportunity or Phylon re-
minded the black reading public of his work as author and editor or
brought news of Carl Van Vechten's attempts to establish a memorial
collection of books and artifacts at the Yale University Library. If
any literary work sustained Johnson's memory during these years, it
was his novel; The Autobiography of an Ex-Coloured Man was reprinted
in 1949 by New American Library, and Hugh M. Gloster and Robert A.
Bone each devoted a dutiful five pages to the book in their separate
literary histories of the Afro-American novel. Johnson's reputation
was certainly at its lowest ebb during these decades.

However, in 1960, somewhat in advance of the resurgence of enthusiasm for black culture and art, a new paperback edition of The
Autobiography of an Ex-Coloured Man, with an introduction by Arna
Bontemps, was issued by Hill and Wang, and in 1965 the novel was again
reprinted, this time with Booker T. Washington's Up From Slavery and
W. E. B. DuBois' The Souls of Black Folk as Three Negro Classics,
edited by John Hope Franklin. These reprintings may have helped to
call attention to Johnson between 1966 and 1976, during which years
two biographies, two special issues of journals, and a large number
of articles on Johnson appeared.

The first of the biographies, Ellen Tarry's Young Jim: The Early
Years of James Weldon Johnson (1967), written for the inspiration of
young readers, was not necessarily a significant gauge of Johnson's
reputation, but this was followed in 1973 by Eugene Levy's scholarly
biography James Weldon Johnson: Black Leader, Black Voice. Between
the publication of these two books, the centenary of Johnson's birth
provided the occasion for memorial issues of The Crisis (June 1971)
and Phylon (Winter 1971). The Crisis features a death mask of Johnson
on the cover, an editorial praising him, a brief biography and a sampling of his own work as well as articles on his roles as N.A.A.C.P.
official, writer, and friend. The special number of Phylon is particularly valuable, offering essays by distinguished black scholars on
Johnson's work as poet, novelist, critic, musician, and journalist.

Most noteworthy of the recent developments in Johnson scholarship,
however, has been the increased recognition of his artistry, especially
as a novelist. In spite of brief comments by reviewers and critics
about the ex-colored man's psychological complexity, most critics before 1970 emphasized the social aspect of The Autobiography of an Ex-
Coloured Man. This tendency to read the book as a tract rather than
as a novel probably inhibited critics' serious consideration of Johnson's techniques as a novelist. Yet in Along This Way Johnson tells
of talking the book over with Brander Matthews soon after he began
work on it, and his comments on the writing of the book reveal a con-
scious literary artist: "The use of prose as a creative medium was
new to me; and its latitude, its flexibility, its comprehensiveness,
the variety of approaches it afforded for surmounting technical dif-
ficulties gave me a feeling of exhilaration...."[4]

Introduction — James Weldon Johnson

In 1971 a group of articles began to explore the artistic dimensions of the novel. Robert E. Fleming offered a reading of the novel as an ironic self-portrait by the first-person narrator, whose Freudian slips and unconscious lapses inadvertently reveal his truest self (1971.B7). Marvin Garrett came to the same general conclusions independently but emphasized Johnson's use of foreshadowing early in the novel to accomplish his purpose (1971.B9). Simone Vauthier followed up these two studies by noting how Johnson mingled the autobiographical and picaresque modes to satirize the American dream (1973.B3), while Stephen Ross suggests that the irony perceived by Fleming and Garrett is directed, not at the narrator, but at the white world and its standards (1974.B9). In another area of criticism, Houston A. Baker (1973.B1) and Robert E. Fleming (1970.B3) have examined Johnson's influence on later black novelists, particularly Ralph Ellison, whose Invisible Man exhibits numerous ties to Johnson's novel.

Both Richard Long's article on Johnson's poetry in Phylon (1971.B13) and Jean Wagner's Black Poets of the United States (1973.B4) contain thoughtful studies of Johnson's progress from poetic conventionality to inventiveness during his career. Blyden Jackson and Louis D. Rubin, in Black Poetry in America (1974.B7), cover much of the same ground with an emphasis on Johnson's unique contributions to the poetic idiom of black American literature. The study of Johnson's poetry has thus far not penetrated as deeply into his works as the studies of his fiction, but a suitable climate for later analyses has been created.

Johnson's emergence from relative obscurity to his place of prominence during the 1920's and 1930's, as documented by book reviewers and popular critics, was due as much to his political position and the social climate of the times as to the character of his literary work. His rediscovery over the past ten years is more solidly grounded on his permanent artistic achievement. Thus, in the future any thorough study of black fiction or poetry must take Johnson's literary contributions into consideration, both for their own merits and for their influences on later writers.

NOTES

[1] James Weldon Johnson, God's Trombones (New York: Viking Press, 1969), p. 7.

[2] Ibid., p. 8.

[3] The Knopf printing changed the title to The Autobiography of an Ex-Coloured Man and used British spelling variants throughout the novel. Except when referring to the first edition, I have used "Ex-Coloured" as the standard spelling. In the annotations I have followed the usage of the source.

[4] James Weldon Johnson, Along This Way (New York: Viking Press, 1933), p. 238.

Writings about
James Weldon Johnson, 1905-1976

1905 A BOOKS - NONE

1905 B SHORTER WRITINGS

1   SIMMONS, R. C. "Europe's Reception to Negro Talent." The
    Colored American Magazine, 9 (November), 635-42.
        Account of the Cole and Johnson musical tour of England
    and the continent in the summer of 1905, chiefly describing
    their reception in London.

1912 A BOOKS - NONE

1912 B SHORTER WRITINGS

1   ANON. "An Ex-Colored Man: A Negro Who Passed as a White
    Tells His Life Story." New York Times Review of Books
    (26 May), Part 6, p. 319.
        While this remarkable story appears to be true, it is
    possible that The Autobiography of an Ex-Colored Man is a
    work of the imagination. Even if it is not all literally
    true, it does offer a great deal of information on America's
    race problem. The author coolly analyzes the waste of the
    white man's energies in perpetuating the racial status quo
    and looks upon the confused white race with something like
    pity.

2   ANON. Review of Autobiography of an Ex-Colored Man. The
    Booklist, 9 (September), 7.
        The author's regrets about having passed for white and
    his keen observations on Negro life help to convince the
    reader that his rather sensational story may be true.

3   FAUSET, JESSIE. Review of The Autobiography of an ex-Colored
    [sic] Man. The Crisis, 5 (November), 38.
        This treatment of "passing" covers nearly every phase of
    the American racial scene in various parts of the country

1912

from New England to the deep South comprehensively and
believably. While it is fiction, it is obviously based on
a thorough knowledge of the problems it presents.

1913 A BOOKS - NONE

1913 B SHORTER WRITINGS

1   ANON. "Men of the Month: A Writer." The Crisis, 5 (February),
     171-72.
         Brief biographical sketch of Johnson stressing diplomatic
     career and varied skills as writer of musical comedy and
     verse. Includes a picture and prints Johnson's poem "Fa-
     ther, Father Abraham."

2   MATTHEWS, BRANDER. "American Character in American Fiction:
     Three Books Which Depict the Actualities of Present-Day
     Life." Munsey's Magazine, 49 (August), 794-98.
         Novels which depend on plot alone do not survive long;
     those which have unforgettable characters have far better
     chances of lasting. Reviews William Dean Howells' New
     Leaf Mills, A Chronicle, Robert Herrick's One Woman's Life
     and Johnson's Autobiography of an Ex-Colored Man. While
     Autobiography is presented as a factual book, it seems to
     Matthews to be fiction. The novel introduces the white
     reader to many areas of life he has never even glimpsed
     before, and as a psychological study it can help white
     Americans understand black Americans. A significant novel.

1917 A BOOKS - NONE

1917 B SHORTER WRITINGS

1   B[RAITHWAITE], W[ILLIAM] S. "The Poems of James Weldon
     Johnson." Boston Evening Transcript (12 December),
     Part Two, p. 9.
         Quotes liberally from Brander Matthews' introduction and
     from "O Black and Unknown Bards" and "Mother Night," two
     poems in the collection. "If we care to regard 'Fifty
     Years and Other Poems' racially there can be no doubt but
     what [sic] it is the most significant accomplishment in
     verse since the publication of Dunbar's poems, that Mr.
     Johnson is the most important poet of the race." However,
     Johnson is intellectually superior to Dunbar and his poetry
     suggests he is free of Dunbar's "sensuality." He should go
     on to distinguish himself as a poet as he has already dis-
     tinguished himself in a number of careers.

Writings about James Weldon Johnson, 1905-1976

2 MATTHEWS, BRANDER. "Introduction" to <u>Fifty Years and Other</u>
  <u>Poems</u>. Boston: The Cornhill Co., pp. xi–xiv.
    Negro poets from Phillis Wheatley on have followed two
  traditions, writing poetry indistinguishable from that of
  whites, and writing racial poetry, much of it in dialect.
  Johnson in this volume follows both traditions. "But where
  he shows himself a pioneer is in the half-dozen larger and
  bolder poems, of a loftier strain, in which he has been
  nobly successful in expressing the higher aspirations of
  his own people." "Fifty Years," in particular, represents
  this group of poems; it is "sonorous in its diction, vigo-
  rous in its workmanship, elevated in its imagination and
  sincere in its emotion."

<u>1918 A BOOKS - NONE</u>

<u>1918 B SHORTER WRITINGS</u>

1 ANON. "Current Poetry." <u>Literary Digest</u>, 56 (March), 36.
    Reprints "Mother Night" from <u>Fifty Years and Other Poems</u>
  and recommends the book.

2 ANON. "The Looking Glass." <u>The Crisis</u>, 15 (March), 186.
    Johnson's first volume of poetry, <u>Fifty Years and Other</u>
  <u>Poems</u>, is a tasteful work and will be a worthy addition to
  any library.

3 ANON. Review of <u>Fifty Years and Other Poems</u>. <u>Educational Re-</u>
  <u>view</u>, 56 (June), 82.
    Recommended as a "unique collection of verse" written by
  a negro and showing both poetic feeling and the skill to
  convey it.

4 ANON. Review of <u>Fifty Years and Other Poems</u>. <u>Catholic World</u>,
  107 (August), 696.
    Johnson's book is one of three reviewed which work "in
  the direction of articulating the American soul in verse."
  The title poem is a noble commemoration of the Emancipation,
  and the other poems are interesting as well.

5 BRAWLEY, BENJAMIN. Review of <u>Fifty Years and Other Poems</u>.
  <u>The Journal of Negro History</u>, 3 (April), 202-203.
    While the dialect poems are worthy of attention, the
  best poems in this collection are "Mother Night," "O Black
  and Unknown Bards," "The White Witch," and "The Young War-
  rior"—notwithstanding the case that can be made for the
  title poem. Johnson has made his mark as a leading poet of
  the race.

1919

1919 A BOOKS - NONE

1919 B SHORTER WRITINGS

1   ANON. Review of Fifty Years and Other Poems. The Booklist,
       15 (February), 171.
          The poem "Fifty Years" commemorates the emancipation and
       like many other poems in the collection is dignified and
       patriotic; others are in negro dialect. Johnson both inter-
       prets his people and argues for fair treatment.

*2   ANON. Review of Fifty Years and Other Poems. New York Call
       (9 February), p. 11.
          Listed in Book Review Digest.

1920 A BOOKS - NONE

1920 B SHORTER WRITINGS

1   ANON. "The New Secretary." The Crisis, 21 (December), 68.
          Tells of Johnson's election, in December 1920, as Secre-
       tary of the National Association for the Advancement of
       Colored People.

1922 A BOOKS - NONE

1922 B SHORTER WRITINGS

1   ANON. "The Looking Glass." The Crisis, 24 (May), 34-35.
          In his preface to The Book of American Negro Poetry,
       Johnson rightfully emphasizes the importance of the Negro's
       contribution, especially through ragtime, to American music
       and poetry.

2   ANON. Review of The Book of American Negro Poetry. The Book-
       list, 18 (May), 276.
          This anthology collects the "conscious self-expression
       of the educated colored race" rather than folk poetry.

3   ANON. Review of The Book of American Negro Poetry. Monthly
       Bulletin of the Carnegie Library of Pittsburgh, 27, no. 6
       (June), 291.
          Brief mention identifying book as an anthology prefaced
       by an "essay on the negro's creative genius."

Writings about James Weldon Johnson, 1905-1976

1922

4   ANON. Review of The Book of American Negro Poetry. The Dial,
    73 (August), 236.
        This collection proves that not only has the Negro "made
    an authentic contribution to American poetry, but that he
    has proved himself a master both of light and serious verse."

5   ANON. Review of Fifty Years and Other Poems. Carnegie Library
    of Pittsburgh Monthly Bulletin, 27, no. 9 (November), 511.
        Brief note on this collection--"poems by an American
    negro."

6   FAUSET, JESSIE. Review of The Book of American Negro Poetry.
    The Crisis, 24 (June), 66.
        Johnson's excellent selection of poets supports his in-
    formative and graceful introduction, in which he contends
    that the Negro has produced the only truly American art.
    The book as a whole strongly documents the genius of the
    American Negro.

7   GUITERMAN, ARTHUR. "Poem, Parody, and Play." The Independent,
    108 (22 April), 396-97.
        Omnibus review including The Book of American Negro Poetry.
    While Johnson's collection serves a useful purpose, much of
    the contents is disappointing as poetry. However, many of
    the more recent poets such as Claude McKay and the editor
    himself show that Afro-American poets are making progress.

8   L., B. Review of The Book of American Negro Poetry. Survey,
    48 (15 April), 89-90.
        "Few if any anthologies of modern American verse excel
    the one before us in the qualities that make for permanent
    value." Sincerity is the one characteristic that unites
    these poems although many are on racial subjects. The Negro
    "has arrived" as a poet, as this volume demonstrates.

9   LITTELL, ROBERT. "Negro Poets." The New Republic, 31
    (12 July), 196.
        The contents of this valuable anthology, The Book of
    American Negro Poetry, are uneven. While many of the poets
    write with true power, especially when writing specifically
    of American racial relations, others are too derivative and
    others too flowery. Not remarkable in a literary sense, the
    collection has considerable value as a human document.

10 REELY, MARY KATHARINE. Review of The Book of American Negro
    Poetry. Wisconsin Library Bulletin, 18 (July), 182.
        Although Paul Laurence Dunbar has been well known, there
    are other negro poets worth knowing. This collection serves
    as an introduction to several.

15

1922

11   WHITE, WALTER F. "Negro Poets." The Nation, 114 (7 June),
        694-95.
        The best part of The Book of American Negro Poetry is the
     40-page preface in which Johnson has done a great deal to
     stake out the place of the Negro in American literature by
     pointing out both the value and variety of his influence on
     general literature and by tracing the history of black poetry
     from Phillis Wheatley to the 1920's. The poetry itself is
     excellent, particularly that of Anne Spencer, Claude McKay,
     and Johnson himself.

12   _____. "The Negro's Contribution." The Bookman, 55 (July),
        530-32.
        In The Book of American Negro Poetry Johnson, "one of the
     two foremost poets of his race and indeed,...one of the few
     worth while poets of America," has taken a major step toward
     acquainting the nation with accomplishments of the race be-
     sides spirituals and jazz. After examining the work of over
     100 black poets, he has presented 31 in this volume of excel-
     lent and varied poetry. While much of the poetry, naturally
     enough, contains propaganda, much transcends race. But per-
     haps the preface is even stronger than the rest--"a liberal
     education on the source of much of the few contributions
     America has made to the arts."

13   WOOD, CLEMENT. "American Negro Poetry." New York Evening Post
        Literary Review (10 June), p. 716.
        Both as editor and essayist Johnson has distinguished him-
     self with the publication of The Book of American Negro Po-
     etry. His choice of poetry, which runs from "primitive dia-
     lect rhymes to the most sophisticated intellectualized po-
     etry," is excellent and can only add to the respect which
     readers have for his race. His critical introduction is
     sound and "arresting." In his own poetry, which the reader
     may find in the anthology or in Fifty Years and Other Poems,
     Johnson proves to be an expert poet as well as critic. One
     can only agree with Dr. Brander Matthews, who says in the
     introduction to the latter volume that Johnson's race is
     fortunate to have him for a spokesman.

1923 A BOOKS - NONE

1923 B SHORTER WRITINGS

1   ANON. Review of The Book of American Negro Poetry. The Jour-
        nal of Negro History, 8 (July), 347-48.
        This valuable book can be useful to the student of his-
     tory both for its introduction and for the biographical

notes on the individual poets. The attitudes and feelings
of the past are revealed in the poetry those times produced.

1924 A BOOKS - NONE

1924 B SHORTER WRITINGS

1 HORNE, FRANK S. "Black Verse." Opportunity, 2 (November),
330-32.
Review of Anthology of Verse by American Negroes (Durham,
N.C.: Trinity College Press, 1924), edited by Newman Ivy
White and Walter Clinton Jackson. By contrasting the book
with Johnson's The Book of American Negro Poetry, it is evident that Johnson has produced a more sensitive and thoughtful anthology.

1925 A BOOKS - NONE

1925 B SHORTER WRITINGS

1 ANON. "The Eleventh Spingarn Medallist." The Crisis,
30 (August), 183.
Reports Johnson's receipt of the Spingarn Medal at the
N.A.A.C.P. annual conference in Denver.

2 ANON. Review of The Book of American Negro Spirituals. The
World Tomorrow, 8 (November), 354.
Johnson's introduction to this large, well-done collection
"gives a most discriminating analysis of the distinctive
qualities of American Negro music and sketches the background from which it developed."

3 BRICKELL, HERSCHEL. "Quaint Negro Folk-Songs Both Sacred and
Secular." New York Evening Post Literary Review (10 October), p. 2.
Johnson's choices are good and the musical settings come
"remarkably close" to the singing of negroes. His introduction to The Book of American Negro Spirituals is an important essay on the significant contributions of spirituals
to American culture in general, and it should be read by
anyone whose experience with spirituals has been limited to
vaudeville shows. "I do not know of another [book] at the
moment that can compare with it...."

4 DuBOIS, W. E. B. "Our Book Shelf." The Crisis, 31 (November),
31.

1925

As a music critic, Johnson shows in The Book of American
Negro Spirituals that he is able to analyze and interpret
the musical art of the Negro. The result is an entertaining
and satisfying introduction which traces the origins and
development of black music. Rosamond Johnson and Lawrence
Brown have done a careful and successful job of recording the
musical arrangements of representative spirituals.

5 KENNEDY, R. EMMET. Review of The Book of American Negro Spirituals. The Saturday Review of Literature, 2 (12 December),
   409.
       Johnson's scholarly introduction and the songs should
   convince doubting critics that the American Negro does indeed have a claim to originality in the creation of his own
   music. J. Rosamond Johnson and Lawrence Brown have done an
   admirable job of maintaining the spirit of the originals in
   their arrangements.

6 LEE, MUNA. "Songs from the Heart of the American Negro." New
   York Times Book Review (18 October), p. 7.
       In The Book of American Negro Spirituals Johnson has col-
   lected sixty-one of the best of his people's spirituals and
   has provided an informative introduction on their origins.
   The songs themselves, with their curious mixture of naiveté
   and beauty, document the eternal hope of the Negro through
   his hardships. Their collection is a valuable service.

7 MENCKEN, H. L. "Hiring a Hall: Negroes' Contribution to Music
   Condensed in a Book of Spirituals." New York World, The Book
   World (15 November), p. 6.
       Because of his musical background, his youth in the South,
   and his race, Johnson was perfectly prepared to collect these
   songs. The Book of American Negro Spirituals is the best
   book so far dealing with Negro religious music. Discusses
   the songs themselves at length.

8 RAMSAY, JANET. "Afro-American Concord." The New Republic,
   45 (30 December), 168-69.
       Johnson's preface to this valuable collection, The Book
   of American Negro Spirituals, is competent but controversial.
   He insists on the African origin of Negro spirituals and
   offhandedly dismisses those critics who would suggest the
   influence of European folk-songs and white revival music.
   However, the music of many of the songs Johnson includes
   seems to bear out his theory, and the songs chosen, whatever
   their ultimate origin, have a rich and varied beauty.

9 VAN DOREN, MARK. "First Glance." The Nation, 121 (16 December),
   [707]-708.

1925

The Book of American Negro Spirituals has become immensely
popular and its success is well deserved. The sixty-one
songs included by Johnson are valuable and worthy of attention. Although Johnson is generally sensible in his introduction, he is offhanded in his contention that the songs owe
nothing to Western tradition. While it is obviously not his
business to trace the origins completely, he could at least
suggest the desirability of future research.

10   VAN VECHTEN, CARL. "The Songs of the Negro." New York Herald
     Tribune Books (25 October), pp. 1-2.
     The Book of American Negro Spirituals is "the newest and
     best" in a series of books which record the music of the
     American Negro. Johnson's introduction gives a thorough
     analysis and history of the origins of the music and should
     prove to be of "inestimable value" to singers and students
     of black music. It is a "simple, sane, able and dignified
     dissertation on the subject, viewed from many angles." J.
     Rosamond Johnson and Lawrence Brown are to be complimented
     for their arrangements. The editors should be encouraged
     to continue their work with black music, perhaps moving on
     to blues and work songs. This collection compares most
     favorably with the two "scholarly" works reviewed with it.

11   _____. "Religious Folk Songs of the American Negro--A Review."
     Opportunity, 3 (November), 330-31.
     Johnson's introduction to The Book of American Negro
     Spirituals is a "clear, logical, and readable" analysis of
     the songs as well as an historical survey. Further, the
     idiom of the original songs has been maintained nicely, as
     it has not been by some who have recorded the lyrics in
     standard English. J. Rosamond Johnson and Lawrence Brown
     preserve the integrity of the music unlike some arrangers
     who have attempted to improve on the originals by making
     them sound more European.

12   WHITE, WALTER. "Negro Spirituals." The Bookman, 62 (December),
     490-92.
     Johnson's introduction to The Book of American Negro
     Spirituals is "interesting and satisfying" as he delves into
     the origins of the spirituals. Knowing the suffering that
     underlies the songs, he brings a sort of understanding that
     no white person could attain. Rosamond Johnson and Lawrence
     Brown are commended for their record of the words and music
     of the sixty-one songs.

13   WOODSON, CARTER G., ed. "Progressive Oratory: James Weldon
     Johnson," in his Negro Orators and Their Orations. Washington:
     Association for Study of Negro Life and History, pp. 663-71.

Writings about James Weldon Johnson, 1905-1976

1925

Biographical sketch and reprinting of Johnson's 1923 speech, "Our Democracy and the Ballot."

1926 A BOOKS - NONE

1926 B SHORTER WRITINGS

1 ANON. Review of The Book of American Negro Spirituals. The Booklist, 22 (January), 148.
Johnson has collected the most "popular and familiar" spirituals and published them with musical arrangements by J. Rosamond Johnson and Lawrence Brown.

2 ANON. Review of The Book of American Negro Spirituals. The Journal of Negro History, 11 (January), 221-22.
Johnson examines Negro music seriously and carefully in his introduction. Though not the first such collection, it does take "a much bolder step...in dignifying Negro music by placing it among the important contributions of modern times."

3 ANON. "N.A.A.C.P. 'Slush Fund' Aired." The Pittsburgh Courier (9 October), pp. 1-2.
News story on the alleged mishandling of funds from the American Fund for Public Services by Johnson and other officials of the N.A.A.C.P.

4 ANON. Review of The Second Book of American Negro Spirituals. The Booklist, 23 (December), 121.
While this collection contains lesser known songs than the first, it is still charming.

5 ANON. "More Negro Spirituals." New York Times Book Review (19 December), p. 24.
Johnson and his brother J. Rosamond Johnson have done a professional, tasteful job in collecting The Second Book of American Negro Spirituals. As Johnson suggests in his introduction, the effect of spirituals on Negro life and on American life in general has been great, and it would be a tragedy to let them pass unrecorded. This collection deserves the same popularity accorded Johnson's first book of spirituals.

6 FRANCIS, WAYNE. "Lift Every Voice and Sing." The Crisis, 32 (September), 234, 236.
Account of the writing of "Lift Every Voice and Sing" by Johnson and his brother, J. Rosamond Johnson. Quotes extensively from a statement made by James Weldon Johnson about the composition of the song and its reception.

7   GUITERMAN, ARTHUR. "Poets of New England and Otherwhere."
    The Outlook, 144 (24 November), 409.
        Mentions The Second Book of American Negro Spirituals in
    review of recent poetry as "a wealth of spontaneous compo-
    sition not to be neglected by those interested in the his-
    tory...of American music."

8   LYON, ERNEST. A Protest Against the Title of James Weldon
    Johnson's Anomalous Poem as a "Negro National Anthem" as
    Subversive of Patriotism. No publisher, 16 pp.
        Attacks the informal naming of "Lift Every Voice and
    Sing" as "Negro National Anthem." Johnson's reply included.

9   NILES, ABBE. "Rediscovering the Spirituals." The Nation, 123
    (8 December), 598-600.
        General discussion of the spirituals as literature.
    Johnson is praised as a collector, but his introductions
    are not historical enough: he should have made efforts to
    find the origins of the songs. The arrangements in the
    first volume were disappointing, but those in The Second
    Book of American Negro Spirituals are highly recommended.

10 REELY, MARY KATHARINE. Review of The Second Book of American
    Negro Spirituals. Wisconsin Library Bulletin, 22
    (December), 330.
        Sixty-one songs are added to the first collection by the
    Johnson brothers.

11 VAN VECHTEN, CARL. "Don't Let Dis Harves' Pass." New York
    Herald Tribune Books (31 October), pp. 4-5.
        Of the two books of spirituals reviewed, Johnson's The
    Second Book of American Negro Spirituals is "by far the
    most important." The introduction is "charming" but John-
    son did so thorough a job in his previous book that there
    was little he could add. J. Rosamond Johnson's arrangements
    are simpler and better than those in the first book. "The
    new collection will be as popular as its predecessor, and
    worthily so."

1927 A BOOKS - NONE

1927 B SHORTER WRITINGS

1   ANON. Review of The Second Book of American Negro Spirituals.
    Carnegie Library of Pittsburgh Monthly Bulletin, 32, no. 2
    (February), 77.
        Brief mention.

1927

2   ANON. Review of God's Trombones. The Saturday Review of
      Literature, 3 (11 June), 904.
          Johnson's "triumph" in the book is that he manages to
      capture the black preacher's manner, as well as his subject
      matter, in free verse without resorting to dialect. "Go
      Down Death" in particular is striking. No student of Negro
      art can afford to miss this beautiful work.

3   ANON. "Poetry and Eloquence of the Negro Preacher." New York
      Times Book Review (19 June), p. 11.
          While Johnson admittedly bases his seven verse sermons
      on the real sermons he has heard in black churches, he also
      shows considerable originality in his poetic renditions.
      God's Trombones shows "sensitivity, artistic judgment, and
      a sustained emotional beauty."

4   ANON. "Better Books for All-Round Reading." World Tomorrow,
      10 (October), 427.
          Brief mention of God's Trombones, describing its contents.

5   ANON. Review of God's Trombones. Carnegie Library of Pitts-
      burgh Monthly Bulletin, 32, no. 9 (November), 590.
          Brief note, describing the physical format of the volume
      in more detail than the contents.

6   ANON. Review of The Autobiography of an Ex-Coloured Man.
      Carnegie Library of Pittsburgh Monthly Bulletin, 32, no. 10
      (December), 627.
          Brief note on the republication of Autobiography, clas-
      sifying the book as a sociological work. Quotes the segment
      of the introduction by Carl Van Vechten which makes it clear
      that the book is not a genuine autobiography.

7   ANON. Review of God's Trombones. The Booklist, 24 (December),
      110.
          Johnson "transcribes" these sermons, an important part
      of negro folklore, in poetic form. They are both dignified
      and spontaneous.

8   ANON. Review of God's Trombones. The Open Shelf (December),
      p. 133.
          Johnson has recorded his memories of the negro preachers
      he knew in his youth in seven verse sermons. The poems have
      a "deeply racial emotional quality and rhythm but are not
      in dialect."

9   AUSLANDER, JOSEPH. "Sermon Sagas." Opportunity, 5 (September),
      274-75.

1927

God's Trombones is a truly unique achievement and Johnson is far too modest when he suggests in his introduction
that he is more or less recording the old black preachers.
The future of the "Renaissance in American poetry" depends
at present on Negro poets, and none is more distinguished
than Johnson. One objection--Johnson's dislike for dialect
is too extreme. It may be used to good advantage by black
poets even though Johnson here chooses not to use it.

10   BENJAMIN, HERBERT B. "Songs for a New Dawn." The Bookman,
     65 (August), 717-18.
       Omnibus review of seven new books of poetry. God's
     Trombones is very well done: the sermons in verse "sound
     too good to be true."

11   BROWN, EVELYN S. "Negro Achievement Revealed by Harmon Awards."
     Opportunity, 5 (January), 20-22.
       Story of the awarding of the first William E. Harmon
     Awards for Distinguished Achievement (in the area of race
     relations). Johnson won a second prize in literature for
     his collections of Negro spirituals; Countee Cullen's Color
     took first prize.

12   CULLEN, COUNTEE. "And the Walls Came Tumblin' Down." The
     Bookman, 66 (October), 221-22.
       Johnson captures the true spirit of the old time black
     preacher in God's Trombones. More important, he has suc-
     ceeded in his intention of replacing dialect with a new
     medium of expressing the black idiom in poetry and of show-
     ing a facet of Negro character hitherto unknown. "The
     Creation" and "Go Down Death" are magnificent poems.

13   DuBOIS, W. E. B. "The Browsing Reader." The Crisis, 34
     (July), 159.
       God's Trombones "blazes a new path toward the preserva-
     tion of the Negro idiom in art." Johnson is wise to avoid
     the "distraction of dialect," and succeeds well in captur-
     ing the Negro preacher's figures of speech. The poetry is
     beautiful and is complemented by the drawings of Aaron
     Douglas.

14   _____. "The Browsing Reader." The Crisis, 34 (November), 308.
       Johnson's Autobiography of an Ex-Coloured Man, first
     published in 1912, has been reissued in a "beautifully
     bound and printed" edition by Knopf, with introduction by
     Carl Van Vechten.

23

1927

15 _____. "Five Books." The Crisis, 33 (January), 152-53.
   J. Rosamond Johnson's arrangements in The Second Book
   of American Negro Spirituals are "striking" and Johnson
   "has written another interesting preface...."

16 GUITERMAN, ARTHUR. "Poems, Opaque, Translucent, and Clear."
   The Outlook, 146 (6 July), 319-20.
   Johnson's free verse rendition of the old-time black
   preacher's sermons in God's Trombones are "genuinely and
   deeply moving." Johnson was wise to avoid the dialect and
   comedy of so much racial writing. The book is the most
   interesting of the thirteen books discussed in this review-
   essay and "the one that most richly deserves a permanent
   place in the library."

17 K., G. Review of God's Trombones. Boston Evening Transcript,
   Book Section (30 July), p. 2.
   Johnson's book of poems comes at a time when negro art
   is being greeted with keen, and well justified, interest.
   The free verse rendering of black preacher's sermons, full
   of phrases reminiscent of the spirituals, captures the
   vigor and rhythm of negro religious songs and preaching.

18 LOCKE, ALAIN. "The Negro Poet and His Tradition." Survey,
   58 (1 August), 473-74.
   It takes a major poet to capture the early Negro preacher,
   and Johnson proves that he is such a poet, especially in
   "The Creation," "Judgment Day," and "Go Down Death." "Con-
   temporary American poetry and art are richer [because of
   God's Trombones], but richer still the prospects of the
   Negro poet and his tradition."

19 MARCH, J. M. "Is Negro Exhorting High Art, Too?" New York
   Evening Post (6 August), Part 3, p. 9.
   While these seven sermons in verse are interesting, their
   value is mainly as bits of folk life recorded, not as true
   art. Johnson has chosen not to use dialect in God's Trombones, and argues vigorously his reasons for not doing so.
   Nevertheless, the sermons would have been more distinctive
   had he presented them as they would be delivered--in dialect.
   As it is, the sermons could be those of any naive evangelist,
   white or black.

20 MELVILLE, J. HERSKOVITS. "More Spirituals." The New Republic,
   49 (12 January), 230.
   The songs in The Second Book of American Negro Spirituals
   are wisely chosen, perhaps even better than those of the
   earlier collection. Rosamond Johnson has kept the accom-

24

paniments more simple than in the earlier book, but there is still a great deal of room for improvement. Although Johnson makes somewhat exaggerated claims for the lasting interest and popularity of spirituals, he has again edited a valuable book.

21 MONROE, HARRIET. "Negro Sermons." Poetry: A Magazine of Verse, 30 (August), 291-93.
       Johnson, who has been known as an editor as well as a poet, publishes the best of his own poetry so far in God's Trombones. He manages to suggest, without using dialect, both the rhythm and the fire of old-time black sermons. While his efforts aren't uniformly successful throughout, readers "should be grateful for this book."

22 MUNROE, THOMAS. "The Grand Manner in Negro Poetry: God's Trombone [sic]." New York Herald Tribune Books (5 June), p. 3.
       Johnson, "who has done fine work in preserving the spiritual songs," has here tried to convey how the old Negro preacher spoke. Although Johnson belittles the artistic shaping he added to the sermons, "one may suspect that he has contributed a great deal to heighten their dramatic force...." "The Creation" is "almost Miltonic." Johnson makes some good points about the deficiencies of dialect in his introduction, but he doesn't quite make a case for discarding "so rich and musical a variant of English." In fact, parts of some poems seem a bit flat, as if the use of dialect would have helped them.

23 OVINGTON, MARY WHITE. "James Weldon Johnson," in her Portraits in Color. New York: Viking Press, pp. 1-17.
       Factual review of Johnson's life to 1927, with emphasis on his musical career and his days as an executive of the N.A.A.C.P.

24 _____. "In Black and White." Survey, 59 (1 November), 164-65.
       Although first published in 1912, Johnson's Autobiography of an Ex-Coloured Man seems very up-to-date in the life it pictures. The novel is both "an engrossing story and a quiet, unprejudiced discussion of the race question."

25 POTAMKIN, HARRY ALAN. "Heavenly Brass." The Nation, 124 (29 June), 721.
       Johnson has attempted to turn folk sermons into genuine poetry in God's Trombones. At times his use of cliches, which are admittedly frequent in folk speech, is annoying and makes his work seem trite. But on the whole the experiment is a success.

1927

26 QUIRK, CHARLES J., S.J. Review of God's Trombones. Catholic
    World, 126 (November), 283.
        Poetic renditions of the sermons of negro preachers
    "make up an arresting and picturesque volume."

27 REELY, MARY KATHARINE. Review of God's Trombones. Wisconsin
    Library Bulletin, 23 (October), 223.
        Johnson has recreated Negro sermons he heard in his boy-
    hood, using verse and capturing the effects without using
    dialect. A beautiful book.

28 THOMPSON, CHARLES WILLIS. "The Negro Question." New York
    Times Book Review (16 October), pp. 14, 16.
        Autobiography of an Ex-Coloured Man, a compelling novel
    rescued from oblivion by Knopf, offers new and unusual views
    of black life in America and of the phenomenon of passing
    for white. Why should a person who is one-sixteenth Negro
    wish to be taken for white? Simply because in the United
    States life for a white is much more comfortable than it is
    for a Negro. Johnson offers keen criticism of white society
    and of his own in this thought-provoking work.

29 WHITE, WALTER. "Play All Over God's Heaven." New York World,
    Metropolitan Section, "The Book World" (19 June), p. 8.
        "Mr. Johnson has opened up an entirely new and immensely
    rich vein of Negro creative genius" with God's Trombones.
    He has taken the southern black preacher, part orator and
    part actor, "and made a notable contribution not only to
    literature about the Negro, but to the literature of the
    whole world."

1928 A BOOKS - NONE

1928 B SHORTER WRITINGS

1   ANON. Review of Autobiography of an Ex-Coloured Man. The
    Booklist, 24 (January), 174.
        This reprint of a 1912 book offers "a keen and dispas-
    sionate commentary on the status of the negro in the United
    States."

2   ANON. Review of Autobiography of an Ex-Coloured Man. The
    Dial, 84 (February), 163.
        Johnson's novel, first published anonymously in 1912, is
    both a fascinating story and the study of a serious social
    problem. God's Trombones, by the same author, "is one of
    the achievements foreshadowed in the autobiography...."

Writings about James Weldon Johnson, 1905-1976

3   ANON. Review of <u>Autobiography of an Ex-Coloured Man</u>. <u>Specta</u>-
     <u>tor</u>, 140 (25 February), 267.
         "Nothing more revealing of the mind of the negro has
     been published since <u>Up From Slavery</u>."

4   ANON. "An Ex-Coloured Man." <u>Times Literary Supplement</u>
     (22 March), p. 207.
         <u>Autobiography of an Ex-Coloured Man</u>, first published in
     1912, has "been much sought after" and was "well worth re-
     publication." As a psychological novel it is "a classic in
     negro literature." Johnson manages to convey his social
     ideas without resorting to open propagandizing--a rare
     ability.

5   SAUL, MARIAN P. "Negro Ability Gaining Recognition Through
     Efforts of Harmon Foundation." <u>Opportunity</u>, 6 (February),
     46-47.
         Johnson is awarded the first prize in literature for
     <u>God's Trombones</u>.

6   THURMAN, WALLACE. "Negro Poets and Their Poetry." <u>The Bookman</u>,
     67 (July), 555-61.
         Capsule history of black American poetry. Johnson is
     mildly praised for transcending commonplace "Methodist hymn
     book" verse with <u>God's Trombones</u>; his other work "contains
     little of merit." The sermon poems, while imperfect, are
     among the best Negro poems yet written. Like Paul Laurence
     Dunbar, Johnson is an important minor poet who may influence
     later writers.

7   W., E. H. Review of <u>Autobiography of an Ex-Coloured Man</u>. <u>The</u>
     <u>New Republic</u>, 53 (1 February), 303-304.
         As a statement of the educated Negro's point of view this
     book--although probably not wholly autobiographical--is val-
     uable. Unfortunately its literary merits are not as great
     as its social value. Even when his material is excellent,
     Johnson fails to treat it to full advantage: one wishes,
     for example, that he had done more with the psychological
     reaction to "passing." While excellent and honest, it could
     be a better book.

<u>1929 A BOOKS - NONE</u>

<u>1929 B SHORTER WRITINGS</u>

1   DuBOIS, W. E. B. "A Poet's Wail." <u>The Crisis</u>, 36 (October),
     349.

1929

> Reaction to a Charleston, South Carolina editorial (in the News and Courier) on Johnson's "Negro National Anthem." Editorial said Negroes should be happy they were slaves; slavery saved them from primitive life. DuBois contradicts this opinion heatedly.

1930 A BOOKS - NONE

1930 B SHORTER WRITINGS

1   ANON. "Johnson, James Weldon," in The National Cyclopedia of American Biography, Current Volume C. New York: James T. White and Company, pp. 488-89.
    Very brief sketch of Johnson's life and works to 1930.

2   ANON. "Survey of the Month." Opportunity, 8 (August), 250.
    Johnson's Black Manhattan, "a history of the Negro in New York," just published by Knopf.

3   ANON. "The Browsing Reader." The Crisis, 37 (September), 313.
    Although the first six historical chapters might have been done by any careful researcher, Johnson comes into his own in the remainder of Black Manhattan as he speaks authoritatively of Negro art and culture in the New York City he has known--a job he does with his characteristic clarity and style.

4   ANON. Review of Black Manhattan. Among Our Books (formerly Pittsburgh Monthly Bulletin), 35, no. 8 (October), 73.
    Note on Johnson's account of "the Negro and of Negro activities in New York City, from the founding of New Amsterdam to the production of Green Pastures."

5   ANON. Review of Black Manhattan. The Journal of Negro History, 15 (October), 501.
    Though a popular rather than a scholarly history, it has much to recommend it. First, it will be read by many people and second, it presents some facts previously unrecorded in histories. Probably the most valuable part of the book deals with the Negro on the stage.

*6 ANON. Review of Black Manhattan. Chicago Daily Tribune (11 October), p. 16.
    Listed in Book Review Digest.

7   ANON. Review of Black Manhattan. The Booklist, 27 (November), 93.

Johnson is in a good position to write of negro activities in New York City, having worked there for years in the fields of art and literature. The book is "vivid" and "exciting," "a valuable contribution to negro history."

8   ANON. "The New York Negro." Times Literary Supplement (6 November), p. 904.
       In Black Manhattan Johnson defends his race, but without bitterness. The general impression is that recently the Negro has made great progress in housing, employment, and the arts.

9   ANON. Review of Black Manhattan. Spectator, 145 (15 November), 741.
       Johnson "displays the common tendency of his race" by exalting "unworthy heroes" such as "jockeys, nigger minstrels, and baseball giants." Nevertheless the book is worthwhile and even admirable.

10   CHAMBERLAIN, JOHN. "The Negro on Manhattan Island." New York Times Book Review (27 July), p. 5.
       Perhaps the strongest parts of Black Manhattan are the sections on black theater and on housing and residential patterns. Johnson knowledgeably traces the three periods of black theater through minstrel shows, musical comedies, and finally to serious drama. He shows how housing has gradually improved, due mainly to the courage of a series of black realtors, and how Harlem has become a black city within a city. This excellent book may be as significant as Johnson's first, The Autobiography of an Ex-Coloured Man.

11   DuBOIS, W. E. B. "James Johnson Sings Praise of Negroes' Mecca." New York Evening Post (12 July), Section 3, p. 5.
       Johnson's first six chapters of Black Manhattan could have been compiled "by any careful student" of history, but in his second section, he speaks with first-hand authority when he writes of black boxers, jockeys, and bohemians, dealing with a milieu he has known, and produces "the best contribution ever made to the history of American Negro art, and especially the drama." Also well done is the third section, an account of more recent events, including those in which Johnson had a hand. "This is a book to be read and enjoyed, covering for the most part a field quite new to Americans, and done in genial almost colloquial English, clear in meaning, and exhilarating in tone."

12   GANNETT, LEWIS. "Before Harlem Was Black." New York Herald Tribune Books (13 July), p. 1.

1930

Johnson shows his great abilities in Black Manhattan as
he moves from "engaging and surprising history" to "sheer
poetry," from dispassionate objectivity to "warmblooded
passion." On the whole, "a book to make black men proud
and to make white men wonder."

13   HANSEN, HARRY. "The First Reader." New York World (11 July),
Section 1, p. 9.
Black Manhattan is "neither a recital of wrongs nor a
preachment" but a worthwhile book on "the achievements and
experiences of the Negro in New York." The book "should
have an excellent effect" on readers who "have associated
the Negro merely with overdrawn pictures of Harlem cafe
life, and with miscegenation." The everyday Harlem presented in the book is different from white America, yet not as
exotic and wild as the night clubs normally seen by whites
slumming in Harlem.

14   RICH, LOUIS. "Black Manhattan." The Bookman, 71 (August),
564-65.
Johnson is obviously knowledgeable about New York and
writes about the Negro's influence on the city with a
scholarly clarity. The black impact on New York sports,
art, entertainment, and lifestyle are revealed thoroughly.
Black Manhattan helps the reader realize just how cosmo-
politan the city is.

15   SALPETER, HARRY. "Harlem Historian, Bookman." New York World
(20 July), Metropolitan Section, p. 7.
Johnson is a sort of historian of the Negro in New York:
"in 'The Autobiography of an Ex-Colored Man' he told the
story of a Negro in New York from an individual, autobiographical point of view; and in 'Black Manhattan'...he has
told the story from a collective, objective, social point
of view." This book avoids the dangers of apology and
boastfulness; it dispels the stereotype of the shiftless
Negro; it admirably records the history of the Negro in
the New York theater.

16   S., J. F. "The Negroes of Black Manhattan." Boston Evening
Transcript (13 August), Part 3, p. 2.
Johnson, a well-known Negro author as well as an executive
of the N.A.A.C.P., presents a historical and artistic study
of his race in New York City. Black Manhattan is a fascinating if sometimes rambling book. It does seem out of balance at times, as if Johnson is giving more space to a particular figure or subject than it deserves. At times, too,
his racial pride overpowers his judgment and he praises

Negroes excessively, as he does with black actors in the
theater section. He might also have done more with the
changes in society caused by the settling of Harlem. "But
for all its discursiveness, reckless enthusiasm and lack
of order, it is valuable, interesting and unique."

17 SPEER, ROBERT E. "Books of Special Interest: The Negro and
    His Future." The Saturday Review of Literature, 7
    (18 October), 248.
        Black Manhattan is a history of Negroes in New York from
    1626 to the present. If the book is to be faulted, it would
    be because Johnson emphasizes the accomplishments of New
    York Negroes and ignores their problems. He could also say
    more about education and religion in the black community.
    On the whole, good coverage of accomplishments in the theater,
    sports, literature, music, and art.

18 WARNER, ARTHUR. "The Negro World's Capital." The Nation, 131
    (1 October), 353.
        Black Manhattan is admittedly less a history than an
    analysis of certain elements of history. Nevertheless the
    book is valuable as a protest against past injustices even
    in this northern city and as a record of black music, drama,
    and literature.

1931 A BOOKS - NONE

1931 B SHORTER WRITINGS

1 ANON. Review of The Book of American Negro Poetry. The Booklist, 27 (May), 419-20.
        Notes republication of the anthology and the addition
   of a number of poets who have emerged since Johnson compiled
   the first edition.

2 ANON. "Survey of the Month." Opportunity, 9 (May), 154.
        News item on Johnson's appointment to Adam K. Spence
   Chair of Creative Literature at Fisk University.

3 ANON. "Collections of Verse: New Edition of 'The Book of
   American Negro Poetry.'" Springfield Sunday Union and Republican (17 May), p. 7E.
        Johnson has revised his ten-year-old anthology to include
   two recent groups of poets--one which displays considerable
   militance and one which asks to be judged only as poets, not
   as Negro poets. Most noteworthy of the new additions are
   poems by Countee Cullen and Langston Hughes.

1931

4   ANON. "New & Special Editions." New York Times Book Review
        (17 May), p. 18.
        Johnson's updating of his ten-year-old anthology The Book
        of American Negro Poetry not only includes the old standards
        of the first edition but a good sampling of the newer poets
        who emerged during the 1920's.

5   ANON. "Books in Brief." The Christian Century, 48 (27 May),
        716.
        Although a revised edition of a book published several
        years ago, The Book of American Negro Poetry has been en-
        larged so much that it is "virtually a new book." Johnson's
        choices have been judicious and his introduction "paves the
        way to a clear understanding of the spirit and value of the
        American Negro's contribution to poetry." The best poetry
        by recent Negro poets is excellent indeed, judged by any
        standards, and the collection is the most complete dis-
        closure of "the soul of the Negro race" available in print.

6   ANON. "Books in Brief." The Nation, 132 (27 May), 589.
        The chief value of Johnson's revision of his 1922 volume
        The Book of American Negro Poetry is in the addition of poems
        by the younger Negro poets who began to publish in the de-
        cade just passed: Countee Cullen, Langston Hughes, Gwendo-
        lyn Bennett, Sterling Brown, and Arna Bontemps. Their work
        is more obviously independent of white critical standards
        than that of earlier poets.

7   ANON. Review of The Book of American Negro Poetry. Wisconsin
        Library Bulletin, 27 (July), 195.
        Johnson's 1922 anthology has been brought up to date by
        adding works of recent poets.

8   BENÉT, WILLIAM ROSE. "Round about Parnassus." The Saturday
        Review of Literature, 7 (4 April), 714.
        Johnson "has made his selections with the taste of a
        true poet and a thorough knowledge of the extant poetry of
        his race." The Book of American Negro Poetry shows the in-
        born sense of rhythm and music of black people.

9   BROWN, STERLING A. "James Weldon Johnson," in The Book of
        American Negro Poetry. Edited by James Weldon Johnson.
        Revised edition. New York: Harcourt, Brace and World,
        pp. 114-117.
        Biographical sketch. As a novelist, Johnson is "analytic
        and prophetic"; his novel has laid the foundation for many
        later books by others. He is a distinguished critic. How-

32

ever, his strongest area is undoubtedly his poetry: here
his inventiveness has resulted in God's Trombones and his
most recent work Saint Peter Relates an Incident, both real
pioneering works.

10   DuBOIS, W. E. B. "The Browsing Reader." The Crisis, 38
(March), 100.
In "Saint Peter Relates An Incident" Johnson has written
a serious and noble satire which is clothed in beautiful
poetry.

11   _____. Review of The Book of American Negro Poetry. The
Crisis, 38 (September), 304.
In this revision of his 1922 anthology Johnson includes
works by the new generation of poets who have emerged during the past ten years. The collection "deserves even
wider circulation than the first edition."

12   KENYON, BRUCE. "The Summer Crop of Verse." Outlook and
Independent, 158 (22 July), 376-77.
Johnson has brought his 1922 anthology The Book of
American Negro Poetry up to date, producing a "good handbook for the average reader. Unfortunately it is not a
collection of the best Negro poetry." More space should
have been devoted to the best black poets, who are often
under-represented and whose best poems are too frequently
not reprinted. Most of the poetry gives the impression that
it would be better if it were set to music, that it does not
stand well on its own.

13   REDMAN, BEN RAY. "Old Wine in New Bottles." New York Herald
Tribune Books (10 May), XI, p. 13.
Johnson's revision of his 1922 anthology The Book of
American Negro Poetry is "one of the most satisfactory, and
richest" books of its kind; it proves that there are no Jim
Crow divisions in poetry.

1933 A BOOKS - NONE

1933 B SHORTER WRITINGS

1   ANON. "They Stand Out From the Crowd." The Literary Digest,
116 (14 October), 11.
Brief biographical profile of Johnson.

2   ANON. "James Weldon Johnson's Careers." New York Times Book
Review (15 October), p. 4.

1933

> Along This Way--a record of Johnson's many careers as
> composer, lawyer, diplomat, and writer--not only presents
> a varied and interesting individual, but reminds us con-
> stantly, sometimes directly but always by inference, of the
> fight that is constantly being waged by the black race.

*3 ANON. Review of Along This Way. Springfield Republican
(22 October), p. 7.
Listed in Book Review Digest.

4 ANON. "James Weldon Johnson." The Crisis, 40 (December), 279.
The publication of Along This Way is "an event of major
importance, both to the nation and to the Negro race." Emphasizes Johnson's achievements in his many careers and reprints several paragraphs from the book, which is most highly recommended.

5 ANON. Review of Along This Way. The Booklist, 30 (December),
119.
Johnson has written a dignified but modest account of
his varied career as teacher, writer, and secretary of the
N.A.A.C.P. It is notable that no matter how famous he became, he was never shielded from racial insults and snubs,
yet he never becomes bitter about such treatment.

6 BRICKELL, HERSCHEL. "Two American Stories." The North American Review, 236 (December), 573.
Along This Way amplifies Johnson's earlier book The
Autobiography of an Ex-Colored Man. Chiefly the story of
Johnson's life, it is also an illuminating commentary on
racial conditions. An excellent book for either race to
read.

7 EMBREE, EDWIN R. "The Best in Brown America." Survey Graphic,
22 (November), 568-69.
Johnson's ancestral history gives Along This Way a rather
dry start, but the story of his own life is "delightful."
The author's "wise and witty philosophy [adds] zest" to
the book.

8 GILLARD, JOHN T. "Autobiography of the New Negro." The
Commonweal, 19 (17 November), 82-83.
Many Americans, accustomed to looking down on the Negro,
will be amazed at this autobiography. Along This Way tells
of a man accomplished in many fields--writing, teaching,
and serving both his race and his nation. Furthermore it
is a subtle indictment of the racial system in the U.S.

1933

"As a teacher, Mr. Johnson has presented his lesson well;
as lawyer, he argues his case convincingly; as artist, he
achieves his effect subtly."

9   GRUENING, MARTHA. "A Distinguished American." The Nation,
    137 (18 October), 452-53.
        Along This Way is a mellow and pleasant autobiography of
    a distinguished man who has conquered the obstacles placed
    in his way by race. However, in spite of its lack of anger,
    the book is a powerful indictment of racial prejudice.

10 REELY, MARY KATHARINE. Review of Along This Way. Wisconsin
    Library Bulletin, 29 (November), 238.
        Summarizes Johnson's many careers but notes that he "is
    best known as a poet." His life story "would be of interest
    whatever the color or race of its author," but since it is
    the autobiography of a negro, it "takes on added importance
    as a contribution to the history of the race in America."

11 VAN DOREN, CARL. "A Citizen of Whom America Can Be Proud:
    James Weldon Johnson, Largely Responsible for the New Negro."
    New York Herald Tribune Books (1 October), vii, pp. 1, 7.
        Johnson shows wit and irony in Along This Way, the story
    of his rich and varied life. Perhaps his most significant
    work so far, work that has taxed all of his many talents, has
    been his position as an executive of the N.A.A.C.P. At the
    same time Johnson was fighting for the political and econo-
    mic rights of all Negroes, he was encouraging the develop-
    ment of a Negro literature with his anthologies and by the
    example of his own writings. "Something has to be done
    about the plight of his race in America, and he has done
    as much as any man alive. His book is almost the whole his-
    tory of the New Negro in the United States." "'Along This
    Way' is civilized in temper, ironical, urbane, deft and re-
    flective." "It is a book any man might be proud to have
    written about a life any man might be proud to have lived."

12 VILLARD, OSWALD GARRISON. "The Chronicle of a Successful Life."
    The Saturday Review of Literature, 10 (23 December), 369.
        Johnson's autobiography portrays him accurately as a man
    of talent and personal charm, but there are moments when it
    is apparent what it means to be a Negro in the U.S. Although
    Southerners will not like Along This Way, it would be a good
    book for them to read. It is important not only as a story
    of one man's life but as a sort of chronicle of Johnson's
    race.

1933

13   W., M. "Contribution of a Negro." Christian Science Monitor
     (11 November), p. 12.
          In Along This Way Johnson, who has sometimes been confused
     with the protagonist of his novel Autobiography of an Ex-
     Colored Man, tells the story of his own many careers as
     writer, lawyer, diplomat, and secretary of the N.A.A.C.P.
     His life, written about in a quiet, reasonable tone, both
     serves as an example to other Negroes and challenges the
     U.S. to put an end to racial restrictions.

14   WOHLFORTH, ROBERT. "Dark Leader: James Weldon Johnson."
     New Yorker, 9 (30 September), 20-24.
          A New Yorker "Profile" on Johnson, emphasizing his char-
     acter--in particular his talents, his versatility, and his
     ability to change rapidly from one successful career to
     another. Also points out his list of "firsts" and his power
     and influence.

1934 A BOOKS - NONE

1934 B SHORTER WRITINGS

 1   ANON. Review of Along This Way. The Journal of Negro History,
     19 (January), 336-38.
          The "worth while" record of Johnson's life, suggesting
     that his greatest success has been as a man of letters, not
     as an educator, lawyer, or civil rights worker.

 2   ANON. "Survey of the Month." Opportunity, 12 (January), 29.
          News item on Johnson's receiving the W. E. B. DuBois
     Prize for Black Manhattan, "the best book of prose non-
     fiction written in the past three years."

*3   ANON. Review of Negro Americans, What Now? Chicago Daily
     Tribune (22 October), p. 16.
          Listed in Book Review Digest.

 4   ANON. "The Negro's Future." New York Times Book Review
     (28 October), pp. 24-25.
          Although Johnson is writing to Negroes, every white
     American should read Negro Americans, What Now? Race re-
     mains the largest unsolved problem of the U.S., and unless
     it is solved, the future of the nation is bleak. Besides
     appealing to the conscience of possible white readers, John-
     son offers suggestions to the black reader--use all helpful
     organizations such as the church and the press, strive for
     education, demolish stereotypes, but above all, never cease
     fighting.

1934

5   ANON. Review of Negro Americans, What Now? The Booklist, 31
      (December), 117.
          Because of the depression, American negroes are facing
      more difficulties than usual. Johnson eschews the extremes
      of Communism and Fascism and suggests steady united efforts
      to secure their basic rights.

*6   ANON. Review of Negro Americans, What Now? Current History,
      41 (December), vi.
          Unlocatable. Listed in Book Review Digest.

7   BALDWIN, ROGER N. "The Dean of Negro Letters." The New
      Republic, 78 (21 February), 54-55.
          Along This Way would be remarkable even were it not the
      story of "a sensitive Negro intellectual faced by the ad-
      versities of American life." Johnson is to be commended for
      his many accomplishments, as documented in this book, and
      for his manner of relating them without excessive dramati-
      zation of the dangers and wrongs he faced.

8   CHEW, SAMUEL C. "O Heart, Rise Not Up Against Me As A Witness."
      Yale Review, 23 n.s. (Winter), 394-96.
          In Along This Way, Johnson writes with humor and light-
      ness, but does not let the reader forget the reality of race
      relations in his country in this excellent story of his own
      life.

9   DuBOIS, W. E. B. "Whither Bound, Negroes?" New York Herald
      Tribune Books (18 November), p. 4.
          In Negro Americans, What Now? Johnson presents a program
      which is not really new in spite of his clothing it attrac-
      tively. Furthermore he does not emphasize the evils of
      segregation sufficiently, nor does he seem to have an up-
      to-date understanding of economics. The real path we must
      take as Negroes leads to the breakdown of capitalism as we
      know it today, hard as that path may be.

10   E., E. R. Review of Negro Americans, What Now? The Saturday
      Review of Literature, 11 (15 December), 375.
          From the poetry he has written in the past--most notably
      in God's Trombones--Johnson moves to a frank discussion of
      race relations in America. The book is direct and succinct,
      and both black and white readers can benefit from it.

11   GALE, ZONA. "An Autobiography of Distinction." The World
      Tomorrow, 17 (4 January), 20-21.
          Summarizes the high points of Johnson's life as presented
      in Along This Way, which is fascinating because of the author's

1934

          ability to interpret the meaning of the events of his life
as well as to record them.

12   REELY, MARY KATHARINE. Review of Negro Americans, What Now?
Wisconsin Library Bulletin, 30 (December), 238.
      Johnson, a negro leader, discusses the future of his race.
"Addressed to negroes but of interest to all who are con-
cerned with the problem."

13   TAYLOR, ALVA W. "A Negro Speaks to Negroes." Christian Century, 51 (7 November), 1419.
      Johnson praises the Negro church, school and press in
Negro Americans, What Now?, addressed mainly to his race,
and urges race pride, use of the vote, and black capitalism
as solutions to the problems of the Negro.

1935 A BOOKS - NONE

1935 B SHORTER WRITINGS

1   ANON. Review of Saint Peter Relates an Incident. The Booklist,
32 (December), 101.
      Lyric poetry and dialect pieces are combined in this
collection, much of which appeared in Johnson's earlier
volume Fifty Years and Other Poems. A number of the poems
are directed specifically at racial questions.

2   G., J. C. "Negro Americans." Boston Evening Transcript
(9 January), Part 3, p. 2.
      Johnson is amply qualified to analyze the problems of
the Negro race, having established his qualification with
a number of books. All the Negro wants, he says, are the
basic rights all other Americans already have. Johnson
feels that the Negro must force the nation to grant these
rights, using the church and social organizations to promote education and pro-Negro publicity. He eschews radical
solutions and Negro Americans, What Now? is a model of cool-
ness and reason.

3   HOLMES, JOHN. "New Poetry from James Weldon Johnson." Boston
Evening Transcript, Book Section (7 December), p. 1.
      Readers who were impressed with Johnson's God's Trombones
may be disappointed with Saint Peter Relates An Incident.
In spite of some very impressive poems such as the title
poem, "Fifty Years," "Lift Every Voice and Sing," and "En-
voy," the balance of the book will add little to the author's

reputation. "Any representation of Mr. Johnson's literary work will be incomplete without this book, however necessary it is to modify critical praise of it as first-rate poetry." Johnson is "a very busy man, whose greatest forces have been directed for the most part elsewhere."

1936 A BOOKS - NONE

1936 B SHORTER WRITINGS

1 BENÉT, WILLIAM ROSE. Review of Saint Peter Relates an Incident. The Saturday Review of Literature, 13 (4 January), 19.
    Johnson is one of the best of modern black poets. His latest book of poetry is full of the fire and originality that marked his earlier volume, God's Trombones.

2 JACK, PETER MONRO. Review of Saint Peter Relates an Incident. New York Times Book Review (12 January), p. 15.
    "In its way" Saint Peter is a readable book, although permeated with racial consciousness. The title poem attracted some attention in a small private edition a few years ago, and "Fifty Years" is also worthy of note.

3 ROSENBERG, HAROLD. "Truth and the Academic Style." Poetry: A Magazine of Verse, 49 (October), 49-51.
    Although the title poem of Saint Peter Relates an Incident and Selected Poems deals with an "outrageous act of public discrimination," Johnson's conservative and academic style does not do his material justice. He is at his best when he is most clearly under the influence of folk music, as in a few of the colloquial poems. For the most part, though, his language is so stiff that his poetry does not move the reader.

1937 A BOOKS - NONE

1937 B SHORTER WRITINGS

1 BRAWLEY, BENJAMIN. "Protest and Vindication," in his The Negro Genius. New York: Dodd, Mead and Co., pp. 206-14.
    Brief biographical account of Johnson. Summary of Autobiography of an Ex-Colored Man, in which Johnson touches "practically every phase of the race question" and anticipates the interests of the Harlem Renaissance. Really at his best as a poet, Johnson has written such distinguished

1937

poems as the title poem of Fifty Years and "Oh Black and
Unknown Bards." His recent autobiography Along This Way
seems a lesser work than his earlier books: in it he is
self-conscious and sometimes condescending.

2   BROWN, STERLING. "Counter-Propaganda--Beginning Realism,"
in his The Negro in American Fiction. Washington, D.C.:
Associates in Negro Folk Education, pp. 104-105.
    Johnson broke much new ground with his only novel The
Autobiography of an Ex-Coloured Man: treating "the 'aristo-
cratic' mulatto, the problem of 'passing,' the Negro artistic world, the urban and European scene," and asserting at
times that in certain respects Negroes "are better than any-
body else." There are solid merits in the novel, even though
it is less a piece of fiction than a vehicle for discussions
of racial questions.

3   _____. "Dunbar and Traditional Dialect" and "Contemporary
Negro Poetry," in his Negro Poetry and Drama. Washington,
D.C.: Associates in Negro Folk Education, pp. 40-41, 68-69.
    Johnson published a number of poems that showed the in-
fluence of Paul Laurence Dunbar in the "Jingles and Croons"
section of Fifty Years and Other Poems. Later, however, he
attacked these early works, realizing their shallowness.
Unlike Dunbar, Johnson never really captured folk life but
only its externals. Johnson achieved real success with the
folk idiom in his later work God's Trombones, where he truly
evokes the rhetoric and the "dignity, power and beauty" of
of the sermons that inspired the poems.

1938 A BOOKS - NONE

1938 B SHORTER WRITINGS

1   AERY, WILLIAM ANTHONY. "James Weldon Johnson: American Negro
of Distinction." School and Society, 48 (3 September),
291-94.
    Stresses Johnson's never-ending commitment to the cause
of civil rights and bettering the race through education.
Also discusses Johnson's accomplishments as an artist--song-
writer, poet, novelist, and polemical writer. See 1938.B2.

2   _____. "James Weldon Johnson: American Negro of Distinction."
Southern Workman, 67 (December), 375-80.
    The same eulogy as 1938.B1 with only a few minor textual
changes.

1938

3   ANON. "Negro Leader Dies in Crossing Crash." New York Times
        (27 June), p. 17.
        Account of Johnson's fatal automobile-railroad train
        collision. Sums up his accomplishments as writer, N.A.A.C.P.
        official, song-writer. Brief biographical sketch of his
        earlier life.

4   ANON. "James Weldon Johnson." New York Times (28 June), p. 18.
        Editorial on the death of Johnson, who is praised as an
        educator, author, and civil rights worker.

5   ANON. "James Weldon Johnson." The Journal of Negro History,
        23 (July), 405-408.
        Unusually thorough obituary of Johnson—actually a very
        sound short biography treating not only the many careers he
        followed but giving such details as the names of many of his
        popular songs and a complete list of his literary works.

6   ANON. "...and sudden death." Survey, 74 (July), 239.
        Notice of Johnson's death and a summary of his career,
        emphasizing his versatility and his devotion to human rights.

7   ANON. "Milestones." Time, 32 (4 July), 43.
        Brief note on Johnson's death and summary of his accom-
        plishments as writer, civil rights worker, and diplomat.

8   ANON. "James Weldon Johnson." New York Age (9 July), p. 6.
        Editorial on death of Johnson, stressing his achievements
        as a pro-Negro propagandist and reminding readers of John-
        son's work for the Age.

9   ANON. "2500 Pay Final Tribute to James Weldon Johnson; Many
        Celebrities At Last Rites." New York Age (9 July), p. 1.
        Account of Johnson's funeral at Salem Methodist Episco-
        pal Church and of funeral oration by Gene Buck, President
        of the American Society of Composers, Authors, and Publish-
        ers, who compared Johnson's achievements favorably with
        those of Booker T. Washington.

10 ANON. "James Weldon Johnson, Negro American." Christian Cen-
        tury, 55 (13 July), 860-61.
        Johnson's career and character effectively contradict
        the theory that the Negro is racially inferior. Johnson
        was teacher, lawyer, musician, diplomat, secretary of the
        N.A.A.C.P., poet. "His death is a loss to his people and
        to the nation...."

1938

11   ANON. "In Memoriam: Addresses delivered in memory of James
       Weldon Johnson." The Crisis, 45 (September), 292-94,
       308-309.
          Texts of five addresses on Johnson by Fiorello H.
       La Guardia, Mayor of New York: Col. J. E. Spingarn,
       President of the N.A.A.C.P.; Ada Scott Dunbar; Walter
       White, Secretary of the N.A.A.C.P.; and William Pickens,
       Director of Branches of the N.A.A.C.P.

12   ANON. "James Weldon Johnson: Brief Biography." The Crisis,
       45 (September), 291.
          Record of the high points of Johnson's life with chrono-
       logical list of his major works.

13   ANON. "The Nation Pays Tribute." The Crisis, 45 (September),
       295-99, 309-10.
          Memorial statements on Johnson by prominent educators and
       public figures along with excerpts of obituaries from some
       fifty newspapers across the nation.

14   BAXTER, J. HARVEY L. "James Weldon Johnson (Three Sonnets)."
       The Crisis, 45 (September), 291.
          Memorial sonnets serving as elegies for the recently
       deceased Johnson.

15   CALVIN, FLOYD J. "The Digest." New York Age (9 July), p. 6.
          Tribute to Johnson as man of letters and activist.

16   [CARTER, ELMER ANDERSON]. "The Editor Says: James Weldon
       Johnson." Opportunity, 16 (August), 228.
          Johnson's death marks a major loss for the Negro and
       the nation. Whatever posterity decides about his literary
       stature, Johnson as a man and as a civil rights worker was
       a major influence on his contemporaries.

17   LOVEMAN, AMY. "James Weldon Johnson." The Saturday Review of
       Literature, 18 (9 July), 8.
          Johnson's death takes from his race one of their most
       impressive representatives and from literature an author
       of varied and distinctive talent. Briefly covers Johnson's
       many careers and the many genres in which he wrote.

18   MILLER, KELLY. "Kelly Miller Writes About: James Weldon John-
       son The Negro Poet Laureate." New York Age (9 July), p. 6.
          In spite of Johnson's fame it should be remembered that
       he gained his reputation largely by appealing to a white
       audience. He "was not a poet per se" but "might fairly be
       called a literary dilettante scribbling prose or verse as

1939

the mode or the occasion required." His "reputation as a
poet and a literary man is secure in the keeping of the
white race, for he uttered nothing base or offensive to
their racial sensibility."

19   VILLARD, OSWALD GARRISON. "Issues and Men." The Nation, 147
        (9 July), 44.
             Mentions Johnson's many achievements as teacher, writer,
        diplomat, and executive of the N.A.A.C.P., but declares
        that his crowning achievement was his own character--his
        ability to maintain his composure through trying situations
        but to fight when necessary.

20   [WILKINS, ROY]. "James Weldon Johnson." The Crisis, 45
        (August), 265.
             Editorial recalling one of Johnson's finer moments as a
        public speaker with the N.A.A.C.P. as a touchstone of his
        ability as a civil rights advocate.

1939 A BOOKS

1   FISK UNIVERSITY, DEPARTMENT OF PUBLICITY. James Weldon Johnson.
        Nashville, Tennessee: Fisk University, 36 pp.
             Contents: Bibliography of Johnson's books. Chronolo-
        gical table of the major dates in Johnson's life. Anonymous
        biographical sketch. Arthur D. Spingarn's "An Appreciation
        of James Weldon Johnson." Carl Van Vechten's "My Friend:
        James Weldon Johnson." Sterling A. Brown's "The Negro in
        American Literature."

1939 B SHORTER WRITINGS

1   ANON. "James Weldon Johnson: A Biographical Sketch," in
        James Weldon Johnson. Edited by Department of Publicity,
        Fisk University. Nashville: Fisk University, pp. [11]-[18].
             Traces the main events of Johnson's life, depending rather
        heavily on Along This Way, and assesses his importance as
        a writer and a civil rights worker.

2   BROWN, STERLING A. "The Negro in American Literature," in
        James Weldon Johnson. Edited by Department of Publicity,
        Fisk University. Nashville: Fisk University, pp. [27]-[36].
             Discusses the stereotypes of Negro characters in works by
        white American authors and the efforts of black authors to
        counter these stereotypes, to present Negroes as fully round-
        ed characters. Within this context Johnson is judged highly

1939

    significant--as a collector and anthologist of black poetry
and spirituals, as a poet, novelist, and essayist, and as
"good friend and counsellor to younger Negro writers."

3   REDDING, J. SAUNDERS. "Adjustments" and "Emergence of the New
Negro," in his To Make a Poet Black. Chapel Hill: University of North Carolina Press, pp. 87-89, 96-97, 120-22.
    Discusses the early dilemma of Johnson when he found that
his raceless poetry was acceptable to the literary world,
while his work on black themes or protest was not. Examines
Johnson's more militant poems such as "Fifty Years" and his
use of the folk tradition as parts of the "New Negro" movement.

4   SPINGARN, ARTHUR D. "An Appreciation of James Weldon Johnson,"
in James Weldon Johnson. Edited by Department of Publicity,
Fisk University. Nashville: Fisk University, pp. [19]-[22].
    Personal recollections of Johnson's character and person-
ality, with special emphasis on his years with the N.A.A.C.P.

5   VAN VECHTEN, CARL. "My Friend: James Weldon Johnson," in
James Weldon Johnson. Edited by Department of Publicity,
Fisk University. Nashville: Fisk University, pp. [23]-[26].
    Warm personal tribute from a literary friend. Emphasizes
Johnson's role as an ambassador from the black race to the
white: "I do not believe any one could know him without
gaining a respect, sometimes an increased respect, for the
Negro."

1940 A BOOKS - NONE

1940 B SHORTER WRITINGS

1   POTTS, EUNICE BLOODWORTH. "James Weldon Johnson: His Legacy
to Us." Opportunity, 18 (May), 132-35.
    Emphasizes Johnson's work in breaking down stereotypes
about black people--through his own literary works, through
anthologies that presented the works of others, through more
direct action as an editorial writer and executive of the
N.A.A.C.P., and finally, through one of his later works,
Negro Americans, What Now? Calls for others to take up Johnson's work and to continue to work against stereotypes.

2   VAN VECHTEN, CARL. "The Proposed James Weldon Johnson Memorial."
Opportunity, 18 (February), 38-40.
    Johnson's friends and colleagues have decided that the
best monument to Johnson would be a bas-relief head of the

author, sculpted by Richmond Barthé, the Negro sculptor, and carrying some of Johnson's verses, to be placed near Central Park in New York City. Contributions are invited.

1942 A BOOKS - NONE

1942 B SHORTER WRITINGS

1 TOWNS, GEORGE A. "The Sources of the Traditions of Atlanta University." Phylon, 3 (Second Quarter), 117-34.
    Historical article on an institution which was important in forming Johnson's intellect and character, written by his former college roommate. Johnson is pictured as one of Atlanta's distinguished graduates.

2 VAN VECHTEN, CARL. "The J. W. Johnson Collection at Yale." The Crisis, 49 (July), 222-23, 226.
    Description of the initial holdings of the Johnson collection, with a tribute to the author by Van Vechten, who established the collection in his memory.

1943 A BOOKS - NONE

1943 B SHORTER WRITINGS

1 BARTLETT, ROBERT M. "They Blazed New Trails: James Weldon Johnson," in his They Dared to Live. New York: Association Press, pp. 42-46.
    Emphasizes the racial slurs and hardships Johnson endured on his way to becoming a successful author.

2 BONTEMPS, ARNA. "The James Weldon Johnson Memorial Collection of Negro Arts and Letters." Yale University Library Gazette, 18 (October), [18]-26.
    Background material on Carl Van Vechten's founding of the collection. Besides containing many general books and artifacts dealing with Afro-American life, the collection is highlighted by presentation autographed copies of all Johnson's books and by pamphlets, clippings, photographs, records, and letters. Article does not include a detailed list of holdings.

1944 A BOOKS - NONE

Writings about James Weldon Johnson, 1905-1976

1944

1944 B SHORTER WRITINGS

1   DESJARDINS, LUCILE. "James Weldon Johnson, Poet and Diplomat,"
     in Rising Above Color, edited by Philip Henry Lotz. Volume
     5, Creative Personalities Series, edited by Philip Henry
     Lotz. New York: Association Press and Fleming H. Revell
     Company, pp. 98-104.
         Inspirational essay on Johnson's hardships in achieving
     success.

1947 A BOOKS - NONE

1947 B SHORTER WRITINGS

1   ISAACS, EDITH J. R. "The Road to Progress," in her The Negro
     in American Theatre. New York: Theatre Arts, Inc., pp.
     15-16.
         Johnson's Black Manhattan tells the story of the "Negro's
     theatre progress up to the time when he wrote as well as it
     could ever be told."

2   OVINGTON, MARY WHITE. "James Weldon Johnson, 1920-1931; We
     Meet the Nation," in her The Walls Came Tumbling Down. New
     York: Harcourt, Brace and Company, pp. 176-243.
         Chiefly treats Johnson's years as Secretary of the
     N.A.A.C.P., with special attention to his handling of the
     Dr. Ossian Sweet murder case in Detroit and the attempts
     to pass the Dyer Anti-Lynching Bill. Also comments on John-
     son's encouragement of younger writers during the Harlem
     Renaissance and on the man's personally.

1948 A BOOKS - NONE

1948 B SHORTER WRITINGS

1   GLOSTER, HUGH M. "James Weldon Johnson," in his Negro Voices
     in American Fiction. Chapel Hill: University of North
     Carolina Press, pp. 79-83.
         Treats The Autobiography of an Ex-Coloured Man as "an
     important precursor of the Negro Renaissance," especially
     of those later novels such as Jessie Fauset's There Is Con-
     fusion and Plum Bun, Walter White's Flight, and Nella Lar-
     sen's Passing. Johnson is a pioneer in presenting a cosmo-
     politan scene, in treating character realistically, and in
     commenting very frankly on the American racial scene.

1951

2   JOHNSON, CHARLES S.   Introduction to The Autobiography of an
    Ex-Coloured Man. New York: New American Library, pp.
    [5]-[7].
        Provides a capsule biography of Johnson, emphasizing the
    difference between the author and his protagonist. Book
    was meant as a "shock treatment" to the white reader, who
    probably took it at face value. Americans who might not
    read a more scholarly treatment of racial questions may
    still read and profit from their fictional treatment in
    this novel.

3   WHITE, WALTER. A Man Called White: The Autobiography of Wal-
    ter White. New York: The Viking Press, 382 pp., passim.
        Personal anecdotes about Johnson by the man who assisted
    him when he was Secretary of the N.A.A.C.P. and succeeded
    him in that office.

1949 A BOOKS - NONE

1949 B SHORTER WRITINGS

1   THOMAS, RUTH MARIE. "Author, Diplomat, and Public Servant:
    A Study of James Weldon Johnson's Writings." Southwestern
    Journal, 5 (Winter-Spring), 58-72.
        Traces Johnson's "humanitarian" attitudes through his
    published works. While he always tried to better the con-
    dition of his race, Johnson also expresses sympathy and
    understanding toward all victims of injustice.

1950 A BOOKS - NONE

1950 B SHORTER WRITINGS

1   ANON. "A Valuable Collection." Negro History Bulletin, 13
    (February), 107.
        Brief account of Carl Van Vechten's presentation of
    James Weldon Johnson Collection to Yale University.

1951 A BOOKS

1   COPELAND, GEORGE EDWARD. "James Weldon Johnson: A Bibliogra-
    phy." M.A. Thesis, Pratt Institute Library School, 29 pp.
        Lists Johnson's published writings, several unpublished
    manuscripts, and a number of secondary articles on Johnson,
    including obituaries.

1951

1951 B SHORTER WRITINGS - NONE

1953 A BOOKS - NONE

1953 B SHORTER WRITINGS

   1   HUGHES, CARL MILTON. The Negro Novelist: A Discussion of the
      Writings of American Negro Novelists, 1940-1950. New York:
      The Citadel Press, p. 35.
         The Autobiography of an Ex-Coloured Man "is the singular
      achievement of the protest literature of the period" and
      later exerted an important influence on the writers of the
      Harlem Renaissance.

1954 A BOOKS - NONE

1954 B SHORTER WRITINGS

   1   TATE, ALLEN. "James Weldon Johnson, 1871-1938," in his Sixty
      American Poets. Washington: U.S. Library of Congress,
      pp. 59-61.
         A checklist, with Library of Congress call numbers, of
      Johnson's books, and of a set of recordings of his poetry.

1956 A BOOKS - NONE

1956 B SHORTER WRITINGS

   1   BUTCHER, MARGARET JUST. The Negro in American Culture. New
      York: Alfred A. Knopf, 306 pp., passim.
         General remarks on Johnson as poet and compiler of
      anthologies.

   2   RICHARDSON, BEN. "James Weldon Johnson," in Great American
      Negroes. Revised by William A. Fahey. New York: Thomas
      Y. Crowell Company, pp. 137-49. Originally published in
      1945.
         Popular summary of Johnson's life and work.

1958 A BOOKS - NONE

Writings about James Weldon Johnson, 1905-1976

1958 B SHORTER WRITINGS

*1   BONE, ROBERT A. "Novels of the Talented Tenth," in his The Negro Novel in America. New Haven and London: Yale University Press.
       See annotation under 1965.B1.

2   BROWN, STERLING A. "Johnson, James Weldon," in Dictionary of American Biography. Edited by Robert Livingston Schuyler and Edward T. James. Volume 22, Supplement Two. New York: Charles Scribner's Sons, pp. 345-47.
       Brief but thorough biographical sketch of Johnson, including comments on most of his writings.

1959 A BOOKS

*1   TATE, ERNEST CATER. "The Social Implications of the Writings and the Career of James Weldon Johnson." Ph.D. Dissertation, New York University.
       According to the abstract in Dissertation Abstracts, 20, part 2 (1959-1960), 1357, studies Johnson's writings from a "socio-economic and political" point of view and comes to the conclusion that Johnson was an important figure as a molder of public opinion among black and white readers and that he "laid the foundation for writers and artists of the early twentieth century, referred to as the 'Negro Renaissance.'" An important study because it treats Johnson's lectures, newspaper articles, and letters as well as his poetry and fiction, and because Tate interviewed Rosamond Johnson, Carl Van Vechten, Sterling Brown, and Walter White.

1959 B SHORTER WRITINGS - NONE

1960 A BOOKS - NONE

1960 B SHORTER WRITINGS

1   BONTEMPS, ARNA. "Introduction" in The Autobiography of an Ex-Coloured Man. New York: Hill and Wang, pp. [v] -ix.
       This novel "is probably, all things considered, the most representative single work of fiction dealing with the Negro in the United States that is now available." In spite of the fact that the mulatto has been a staple in Afro-American fiction, Johnson's work has outlasted most, probably because of his "sharp insights, his definitive understanding of the 'problem,' and his broad human sympathy...."

1960

2   COLLIER, EUGENIA W. "James Weldon Johnson: Mirror of Change."
     Phylon, 21 (Winter), 351-59.
         Between the turn of the century and the 1920's black
     poetry employing folk materials shifted from the dialect
     poetry of the Paul Laurence Dunbar school to a more subtle
     use of black idiom. Johnson, who wrote dialect poetry and
     a newer form of folk poetry, reflects the changes that took
     place over some thirty years--a period that is extremely
     important in the history of black poetry. Examines Johnson's
     dialect verse as compared to Dunbar's and moves on to John-
     son's experiments--partly inspired by the spirituals and
     partly by Whitman--in God's Trombones.

1961 A BOOKS - NONE

1961 B SHORTER WRITINGS

1   ANON. "Negro National Hymn." Negro Heritage, 1 [April], 9.
         Retells the story of Johnson's composition of "Lift Every
     Voice and Sing," depending on his own account in Along This
     Way.

1962 A BOOKS - NONE

1962 B SHORTER WRITINGS

1   TATE, ERNEST C. "Sentiment and Horse Sense: James Weldon
     Johnson's Style." Negro History Bulletin, 25 (April),
     152-54.
         Reprints a long humorous letter and poem on the Georgia
     mule, written by Johnson to Rosamond Johnson while the
     former was teaching in rural Georgia during a summer vaca-
     tion. Shows a side of Johnson not normally seen in his
     published writing--almost comparable to parts of Mark
     Twain's Roughing It.

1963 A BOOKS - NONE

1963 B SHORTER WRITINGS

1   MEIER, AUGUST. Negro Thought in America, 1880-1915. Ann
     Arbor, Michigan: University of Michigan Press, pp. 79,
     184, 252, 254-55, 257, 268, 269-70, 271.
         Johnson's roles as political leader, song writer, and
     novelist are discussed briefly as they fit into the intel-
     lectual life of his period.

1964 A BOOKS - NONE

1964 B SHORTER WRITINGS

1   BRONZ, STEPHEN H.   "James Weldon Johnson," in his Roots of
    Negro Racial Consciousness, the 1920's: Three Harlem
    Renaissance Authors.   New York: Libra Publishers, Inc.,
    pp. 18-46.
        Discusses Johnson's life and career as civil rights
    activist and treats most of his important works: The Auto-
    biography of an Ex-Coloured Man, Fifty Years and Other Poems,
    God's Trombones, "St. Peter Relates an Incident of the Resur-
    rection Day," and Negro Americans, What Now?   Johnson's
    main mission in all that he did and wrote was to further his
    race and "gain for them a more just share of America's
    opportunities."   Thus, while he never produced really great
    literature, he achieved his own objectives.

1965 A BOOKS - NONE

1965 B SHORTER WRITINGS

1   BONE, ROBERT A.   "Novels of the Talented Tenth," in his The
    Negro Novel in America.   Revised edition.   New Haven and
    London: Yale University Press, pp. 45-49.
        That Johnson "is the only true artist among the early
    Negro novelists" Bone attributes to his early experience
    as a writer of musical comedy.   Autobiography of an Ex-
    Coloured Man is particularly strong in its tone, which
    skillfully mingles tragedy with irony.   Because of his em-
    phasis on Bohemian life in New York and because he empha-
    sizes art over racial protest, Johnson is often considered
    a forerunner of the Harlem Renaissance.   "Yet even Johnson
    cannot wholly repress a desire to educate the white folks"
    and stops the dramatic action of the novel from time to
    time to discuss racial problems.

2   FRANKLIN, JOHN HOPE.   "Introduction" to Three Negro Classics.
    Edited by John Hope Franklin.   New York: Avon Books,
    pp. vii-xxi.
        Brief biographical sketch of Johnson.   Review of his
    literary career.   The Autobiography of an Ex-Coloured Man
    is significant because, although William Wells Brown and
    Charles W. Chesnutt had both treated the light-skinned
    Negro, Johnson's work was the first "to deal primarily with
    the problem of 'passing.'"   In addition, the range of Negro
    life which it describes has been socially important to
    readers and critics.

1966

1966 A BOOKS - NONE

1966 B SHORTER WRITINGS

1 ANON. Review of Along This Way. Bibliographical Survey: The
   Negro in Print, 1, no. 5 (January), 11.
        Informative autobiography of a writer who was also a teach-
   er, principal, college professor, musician, diplomat, and
   N.A.A.C.P. executive.

2 BONTEMPS, ARNA. "The Negro Contribution to American Letters,"
   in The American Negro Reference Book. Edited by John P.
   Davis. Englewood Cliffs, N.J.: Prentice-Hall, Inc.,
   pp. 858, 872-73.
        Stresses Johnson's importance and influence as both poet
   and novelist.

3 LITTLEJOHN, DAVID. "Before Native Son: The Dark Ages" and
   "Before Native Son: The Renaissance and After," in his
   Black on White: A Critical Survey of Writing by American
   Negroes. New York: Viking Press, pp. 23-29, 41-43.
        Johnson is noteworthy for his Along This Way, "one of the
   more dependable and readable of Negro leaders' autobiographies" and for the poems in God's Trombones, which made a
   stir in their day but may look condescending from our vantage point. The Autobiography of an Ex-Coloured Man continues to be read, but it is "more of a social phenomenon than
   a novel." The story line of the novel is "artless, unstruc-
   tured, [and] unselective," but the novel continues to have
   some slight value for the digressive essays that are spread
   throughout the whole. Black Manhattan records somewhat
   interestingly the Harlem Johnson knew.

1967 A BOOKS

1 TARRY, ELLEN. Young Jim: The Early Years of James Weldon Johnson. New York: Dodd, Mead and Company, 230 pp.
        Biography intended for younger readers. Covers the years
   from Johnson's birth to 1901, when he left Jacksonville for
   a career as a song-writer in New York City. The remainder
   of his career is sketched in a twenty-page epilogue. Among
   the illustrations are three pages of manuscript in facsimile
   from the James Weldon Johnson Collection at Yale.

1967 B SHORTER WRITINGS

1 ADELMAN, LYNN. "A Study of James Weldon Johnson." The Journal
   of Negro History, 52 (April), 128-45.

1967

Brief biographical study, emphasizing Johnson's problems
and his responses to them. Points out that the period of
Johnson's life, 1871-1938, was one of considerable racial
turbulence; then shows how Johnson achieved noteworthy status
as educator, attorney, writer, diplomat, and finally executive of the N.A.A.C.P. Emphasis is chiefly on Johnson's
interaction with society and not on Johnson as a man of letters although his writing is touched on.

2 APTHEKER, HERBERT. "DuBois on James Weldon Johnson." The
Journal of Negro History, 52 (July), 224-27.
Prints, with an introduction, the text of a hitherto un-
published address given by W. E. B. DuBois at a dinner in
honor of Johnson on his retirement as Executive Secretary of
the N.A.A.C.P. DuBois emphasizes Johnson's many talents and
his unstinting devotion to the cause of race relations.

3 COPANS, SIM. "James Weldon Johnson et le Patrimoine Culturel
des Noirs Africains." Cahiers de la Compagnie Madeleine
Renaud--Jean Louis Barrault, 61 (May-June), 42-48.
Discursive discussion of Johnson's role as a promoter of
Afro-American poetry and music, especially the latter, and
the roots of black music in Africa.

4 CRUSE, HAROLD. "Harlem Background," in his The Crisis of the
Negro Intellectual. New York: William Morrow, pp. 33-39.
Although Johnson wrote one novel and distinguished himself
as a poet, Black Manhattan and Along This Way are actually
his most important works from our current vantage point.
Unfortunately, these two books reveal that Johnson, an important figure in the Harlem Renaissance, failed to realize
what was at stake. The roles played both by white patrons
of the arts and white artists seeking to exploit Negro
materials were seen as healthy signs by Johnson when actually
they threatened the artistic integrity of the black artists.
Mentions Johnson briefly in various other parts of the book.

5 KELLOGG, CHARLES FLINT. NAACP: A History of the National
Association for the Advancement of Colored People. Baltimore: The Johns Hopkins Press, 332 pp., passim.
Includes a well-documented account of Johnson's extensive
role in the organization.

6 MITCHELL, LOFTEN. Black Drama. New York: Hawthorn Books, Inc.,
pp. 25, 40, 47, 63, 69, 186.
Brief comments on Johnson's part in black theater during
his musical comedy career, 1902-1906.

1967

7   OTTLEY, ROI and WILLIAM J. WEATHERBY, eds. The Negro in New
    York: An Informal Social History. New York: The New York
    Public Library, 328 pp., passim.
        Frequent brief references to Johnson's role in New York
    City history, as man of letters and political activist.

1968 A BOOKS - NONE

1968 B SHORTER WRITINGS

1   JACKSON, MILES M., Jr. "Literary History: Documentary Side-
    lights. James Weldon Johnson and Claude McKay." Negro
    Digest, 17 (June), 25-29.
        Reprints three letters from Johnson to McKay, dating from
    26 January 1928 to 26 March 1937, and quotes one reply from
    McKay to Johnson. Johnson makes extensive comments on McKay's
    work, especially A Long Way From Home.

2   _____. "Letters to a Friend: Correspondence From James Weldon
    Johnson to George A. Towns." Phylon, 29 (Summer), 182-98.
        A selection of letters from the Negro Collection, Trevor
    Arnett Library, Atlanta University. Towns was Johnson's col-
    lege roommate and a life-long friend who taught English at
    Atlanta for 27 years. Letters span the years 1896 to 1934
    and offer some rather surprising insights into Johnson's
    egotism. One letter dated 10 August 1912 offers Johnson's
    comments on The Autobiography of an Ex-Coloured Man.

3   JAHN, JANHEINZ. Neo-African Literature: A History of Black
    Writing. New York: Grove Press, 302 pp., passim.
        Johnson's contributions in fiction, poetry, and the preser-
    vation of folklore are briefly mentioned.

4   KAISER, ERNEST. Introduction to Black Manhattan. New York:
    Arno Press, pp. [5]-[7].
        Johnson's research in Black Manhattan is thorough, bring-
    ing to light a number of relatively unknown facts about slave
    revolts in 1712 and 1742, the founding of Freedom's Journal,
    the first American Negro newspaper, the founding of the
    N.A.A.C.P., and the Harlem Renaissance. But the most im-
    portant contribution of the book is its history of the Negro
    and the theatre in New York City.

5   KELLER, FRANCES RICHARDSON. "The Harlem Literary Renaissance."
    North American Review, n.s. 5 (May-June), 29-34.

Discusses the Harlem Renaissance as a period of image-building among black Americans, with emphasis on Johnson, Claude McKay, Langston Hughes. For years whites had defined the "Negro"; now a group of black artists chose to define their own people. While no one image emerged from the period, it did make clear the need for a new one.

6   LEVY, EUGENE. "Ragtime and Race Pride: The Career of James Weldon Johnson." Journal of Popular Culture, 1 (Spring), [357]-70.
    Biographical treatment of Johnson's career in song-writing and musical comedy. Attempts to reconcile his early impulses toward awakening race pride with his career as a writer of "coon songs." Gradually, in their own songs, the Johnson brothers moved from the derogatory racial stereotypes that had prevailed when they came to New York and began to produce a more assimilated type of music.

7   MARGOLIES, EDWARD. "The First Forty Years: 1900-1940," in his Native Sons: A Critical Study of Twentieth-Century Negro American Authors. Philadelphia and New York: J. B. Lippincott Company, pp. 25-27.
    The Autobiography of an Ex-Coloured Man is "by far the best novel produced by a Negro prior to the 1920's" chiefly because of Johnson's strength as a stylist and the thematic unity of the novel. Also interesting are the sharp pictures of Negro life in various areas of the country. Like too many of his contemporaries, Johnson strays from his plot and into propaganda from time to time. His other notable work is God's Trombones, which is not a complete failure, but is "antiseptic" in its interpretation of Southern folk sermons.

1969 A BOOKS - NONE

1969 B SHORTER WRITINGS

1   ANON. "Trumpets of the Lord." America, 120 (17 May), 599.
    Notes that the musical show Trumpets of the Lord is advertised as being based on Johnson's God's Trombones but that "the relationship is rather tenuous" since the two works have little more than subject matter in common.

2   BOND, FREDERICK W. "Drama with Less Restriction," in his The Negro and the Drama. Originally published in 1940. College Park, Maryland: McGrath Publishing Company, pp. 39-41.
    A brief account of Johnson's early career as a writer of musical comedy, largely dependent on Along This Way.

1969

3   FULLINWIDER, S. P.   "Marginal Men," in his The Mind and Mood
      of Black America: 20th Century Thought.   Homewood, Illinois:
      The Dorsey Press, pp. 85-91.
         One of Johnson's chief motivations in all that he wrote
      was "to promote and popularize the idea that the Negro has
      a unique racial genius" and that he has contributed "the
      only true art of America" to the national culture.   Thus,
      in The Autobiography of an Ex-Coloured Man he exalts black
      music, while in God's Trombones he elevates black preaching
      to an art.

4   KOSTELANETZ, RICHARD.   "The Politics of Passing: The Fiction
      of James Weldon Johnson."   Negro American Literature Forum,
      3 (March), 22-24, 29.
         Although Johnson's sole novel The Autobiography of an
      Ex-Coloured Man treats a subject common to early Afro-Ameri-
      can fiction, he adds to the tradition by injecting the musi-
      cal tradition of the blues--"the blues of being white but
      black."

5   ROBINSON, WILHELMINA S.   "Johnson, James Weldon: Author and
      Diplomat," in her Historical Negro Biographies.   New York:
      Publishers Company, Inc., pp. 213-14.
         Brief biographical sketch of Johnson and descriptions of
      some of his better known works.

1970 A BOOKS - NONE

1970 B SHORTER WRITINGS

1   AMANN, CLARENCE A.   "Three Negro Classics: An Estimate."
      Negro American Literature Forum, 4 (Winter), 113-19.
         Comparative evaluation of the three works included in
      John Hope Franklin's collection: Up From Slavery, The Souls
      of Black Folk, and The Autobiography of an Ex-Coloured Man.
      "It is difficult to discover much to recommend [Johnson's
      novel]." It is "timid" in its content, "sketchy and super-
      ficial" in its form. Both Up From Slavery and Autobiography
      suffer by comparison with DuBois' Souls, the only true clas-
      sic of the three.

2   DANIEL, PETE.   "Black Power in the 1920's: The Case of Tuskegee
      Veterans Hospital." Journal of Southern History, 36 (August),
      [368]-88.
         Account of a conflict (1921-1924) over the staffing of a
      black veterans hospital at Tuskegee. Local whites wanted it

run by whites; blacks, including representatives of the
N.A.A.C.P., wanted an all-black staff. Johnson was involved
as Executive Secretary. After 7 July 1924, staff was completely black.

3   FLEMING, ROBERT E. "Contemporary Themes in Johnson's Autobiogra-
    phy of an Ex-Coloured Man." Negro American Literature Forum,
    4 (Winter), 120-24, 141.
        Johnson has been a seminal novelist who introduced themes
    employed by later Afro-American novelists such as Ralph Elli-
    son, James Baldwin, Richard Wright, William Demby, Ann Petry,
    and John A. Williams. Treats four themes at length: the
    nameless protagonist, racial self-hatred, the black mother,
    and the white patron/white liberal. Suggests other themes:
    flight to Europe, militance vs. accommodation, and white
    standards vs. black standards.

4   JACKSON, MILES, Jr. "James Weldon Johnson." Black World, 19
    (June), 32-34.
        Brief review of Johnson's career, especially as a writer.
    Quotes from the same letters reproduced in Jackson, 1968.B2.
    Essentially, this is a popularization of 1968.B2.

5   WILLIAMS, KENNY J. They Also Spoke: An Essay on Negro Liter-
    ature in America, 1787-1930. Nashville: Townsend Press,
    320 pp., passim.
        Discusses Johnson's part in shaping traditions in poetry
    and the novel and in the editing of folk songs and poetry.
    Also recommends Black Manhattan and Along This Way for their
    historical value.

1971 A BOOKS - NONE

1971 B SHORTER WRITINGS

1   ANON. "James Weldon Johnson." The Crisis (James Weldon John-
    son Centennial Issue), 78 (June), 112.
        Editorial praising Johnson for his part in the civil
    rights struggle and for his literary achievements, and for
    his character.

2   BACOTE, CLARENCE A. "James Weldon Johnson and Atlanta Univer-
    sity." Phylon (James Weldon Johnson Centenary Issue), 32
    (Winter), 333-43.
        An account of Johnson's years at Atlanta as a high school
    and college student. Relies largely on Along This Way.

Writings about James Weldon Johnson, 1905-1976

1971

3 BARDOLPH, RICHARD. The Negro Vanguard. First published 1959.
   Westport, Connecticut: Negro Universities Press, pp. 79,
   134, 139, 140, 151, 153, 175, 217.
   Biographical facts are collected and compared with statis-
   tics on Johnson's black contemporaries.

4 CARROLL, RICHARD A. "Black Racial Spirit: An Analysis of
   James Weldon Johnson's Critical Perspective." Phylon
   (James Weldon Johnson Centenary Issue), 32 (Winter), 344-64.
   In his poetry criticism Johnson treats practical matters
   rather than abstract questions. Examining his prefaces and
   critical articles yields four main critical principles about
   the black poet: (1) Black people have made major cultural
   contributions; (2) Black writers should deal with black
   material; (3) Black culture is unique and its uniqueness
   should be conveyed by black writers; and (4) Black poets
   should experiment with new forms of expression to convey
   the uniqueness of black culture. In Johnson's era this
   meant abandoning dialect poetry for new modes of expression.

5 CURRENT, GLOSTER B. "James Weldon Johnson: Freedom Fighter."
   The Crisis (James Weldon Johnson Centennial Issue), 78
   (June), 116-18, 129-30.
   Sums up Johnson's career with the N.A.A.C.P., from 1916
   to 1930, first as field secretary, then as executive secretary. Emphasizes both Johnson's courage and his ability to
   get results--by protest, marches, propaganda, and personal
   lobbying.

6 COLLIER, EUGENIA. "The Endless Journey of an Ex-Coloured Man."
   Phylon (James Weldon Johnson Centenary Issue), 32 (Winter),
   365-73.
   The narrator's physical journey from South to North and
   back again, to Europe and back, is paralleled by a psychological journey from whiteness to blackness and back again.
   But unlike his literal journeys, the narrator's psychological
   journey does not end: at the conclusion of the novel he is
   still not completely satisfied with his assumed racial identity. Johnson broke a great deal of new ground with his
   novel. It is a precursor of the novels of the Harlem
   Renaissance. Even more important the book stands as perhaps the best examination yet of the dual character of the
   Afro-American.

7 FLEMING, ROBERT E. "Irony as a Key to Johnson's The Autobiography of an Ex-Coloured Man." American Literature, 43 (March),
   83-96.

1971

Sociological readings of Johnson's Autobiography have
obscured his artistic achievement in the novel. Rather
than take it at face value, this analysis reads it as an
ironic character study of a naive protagonist who tells his
story while misinterpreting its significance. The perceptive reader thus responds to the narrator's statements on
a dual level--both for what they say on the surface and for
what they unwittingly tell about the true character of the
narrator. The novel marks a departure from earlier propaganda techniques and introduces more artistic directions
for the black novelist to take.

8   GALLAGHER, BUELL G. "James Weldon Johnson: Man of Letters."
     The Crisis (James Weldon Johnson Centennial Issue), 78
     (June), 119-22.
         A record of Johnson's development as a writer, largely
     dependent on Along This Way, rather than an analytical read-
     ing of specific works. Praises "Lift Every Voice and Sing,"
     Autobiography of an Ex-Coloured Man, and especially God's
     Trombones.

9   GARRETT, MARVIN P. "Early Recollections and Structural Irony
     in The Autobiography of an Ex-Coloured Man." Critique:
     Studies in Modern Fiction, 13 [December], 5-14.
         Johnson's novel centers around the subtle and ironic psy-
     chological portrait of "a morally obtuse and self-centered
     character," the narrator. One of Johnson's chief tools
     for introducing the character and foreshadowing his later
     moral failures is the second chapter, in which the narrator
     tells of his early recollections--incidents which estab-
     lish his characteristic avoidance of pain, denial of guilt,
     and self-pity. The incidents illustrating these character-
     istics in his childhood are repeated with variations in his
     later life until at the end of the novel, the narrator comes
     close to recognizing his own failure. He draws back from
     self-condemnation but only after the reader has had a chance
     to perceive his character and his errors.

10   HUGGINS, NATHAN IRVIN. Harlem Renaissance. New York: Oxford
     University Press, 343 pp., passim.
         Relies rather heavily on Johnson's Black Manhattan and
     Along This Way for information on New York and the Harlem
     Renaissance. Comments on Autobiography of an Ex-Colored
     Man, in which he sees Johnson deploring the tragedy surround-
     ing the loss of black culture. But though Johnson had the
     best of motives, he still was mistaken in believing that
     folk art had to be elevated to high art in order to be
     meaningful, as he shows in his prefaces to the Book of
     American Negro Poetry and God's Trombones.

Writings about James Weldon Johnson, 1905-1976

1971

11 HUNTER, CHARLAYNE. "Widow Says Reawakening of Interest in Work Can Inspire Negro Children." New York Times (12 October), p. 48.
An interview with Grace Nail Johnson on the continuing significance of her late husband's writing. Mrs. Johnson expressed the opinion that Johnson's books were being more widely read than ever on the centennial of his birth.

12 LOGAN, RAYFORD W. "James Weldon Johnson and Haiti." Phylon (James Weldon Johnson Centenary Issue), 32 (Winter), 396-402.
Johnson's four articles for The Nation in 1920 were not only the foundation of a movement to change American policy toward Haiti but also the basis for virtually all subsequent histories of the occupation of Haiti. Equipped with a knowledge of French and of Haitian history, Johnson was a keen observer who soon came to understand that the occupation had great economic advantages for U.S. banking interests and the bureaucrats who administered the occupation. He also exposed racial prejudice by the occupying forces as a severe problem. Although there was no immediate effect, public opinion on Haiti was influenced by the articles and a court of inquiry was convened.

13 LONG, RICHARD A. "A Weapon of My Song: The Poetry of James Weldon Johnson." Phylon (James Weldon Johnson Centenary Issue), 32 (Winter), 374-82.
Johnson's poetry shows a dual development over the years. In form, he moves from his early practice of dividing up his verse between poems in standard English and lesser poems in dialect to writing poems in a new free-verse form that captures the idiom of black speech. In content, he moves from apologetic verse of the Phillis Wheatley school to a militant stand perhaps best exemplified by his satire "Saint Peter Relates an Incident of the Resurrection Day." Johnson's habit of revising his early poems as his poetic credo changed emphasizes the differences between his early and late conceptions of poetry.

14 McPHERSON, JAMES M., LAURENCE B. HOLLAND, JAMES M. BANNER, NANCY J. WEISS, and MICHAEL D. BELL. Blacks in America: Bibliographical Essays. Garden City, New York: Doubleday and Company, 430 pp., passim.
Cites Johnson's works repeatedly under headings such as the N.A.A.C.P., the Harlem Renaissance, Black Poetry, Blacks and the American Theater, and Soul Music.

1972

15   PLOSKI, HARRY A., OTTO J. LINDENMEYER, ERNEST KAISER, eds.
      "James Weldon Johnson--1871-1938. Poet, lyricist, critic,"
      in Reference Library of Black America. New York: Bell-
      wether Publishing Company, Book III, p. 21.
           Brief account of Johnson's life and works.

16   WESLEY, CHARLES H., JAMES ALLEN EGERT, and RICHETTA G. RANDOLPH.
      "Yes, We Knew James Weldon Johnson." The Crisis (James
      Weldon Johnson Centennial Issue), 78 (June), 123-24.
           Personal recollections of Johnson set down by a distin-
      guished black historian, an N.A.A.C.P. executive, and John-
      son's former secretary.

17   WHALUM, WENDELL PHILLIPS. "James Weldon Johnson's Theories
      and Performance Practices of Afro-American Folksong." Phylon
      (James Weldon Johnson Centenary Issue), 32 (Winter), 383-95.
           Johnson was a pioneer in the study of black folk music
      whose two collections of spirituals and the prefaces he
      wrote for them mark a turning point in the understanding
      of black music. Not only did he collect the songs, but he
      brought to them a scholarly approach that allowed him to
      make meaningful generalizations about the qualities of the
      music.

1972 A BOOKS

*1   MILLICAN, ARTHENIA BATES. "James Weldon Johnson: In Quest of
      an Afrocentric Tradition for Black American Literature."
      Ph.D. dissertation, Louisiana State University.
           According to the abstract in Dissertation Abstracts
      International, 33:2385 A - 2386 A, treats Johnson as a pre-
      cursor of the Harlem Renaissance who made important contri-
      butions to poetry and the novel.

1972 B SHORTER WRITINGS

1   BONTEMPS, ARNA, ed. The Harlem Renaissance Remembered: Essays
      Edited with a Memoir. New York: Dodd, Mead and Company,
      310 pp., passim.
           Brief glimpses of Johnson and the part he played in the
      Harlem Renaissance. His roles as poet, novelist, and critic
      are noted but not extensively discussed.

*2   BROWN, MICHAEL ROBERT. "Five Afro-American Poets: A History
      of the Major Poets and Their Poetry in the Harlem Renais-
      sance." Ph.D. dissertation, University of Michigan.

1972

According to the abstract in <u>Dissertation Abstracts</u>
<u>International</u>, 32:3990A, discusses the poetry of Johnson
(and that of Claude McKay, Jean Toomer, Countee Cullen and
Langston Hughes) from a literary, biographical, and historical standpoint. Intended as a guide to introduce teachers
and prospective teachers to significant black poets.

3   LOMAX, MICHAEL L.   "Fantasies of Affirmation: The 1920's Novel
of Negro Life." <u>College Language Association Journal</u>, 16
(December), 232-46.
Discussion of the artistic assumptions behind the black'
novel during the Harlem Renaissance. Johnson's "Race Prejudice and the Negro Artist," <u>Harper's</u>, 157 (November 1928),
769-70; and his "Dilemma of the Negro Author," <u>American</u>
<u>Mercury</u>, 15 (December 1928), 4, are both discussed briefly
in this context.

<u>1973 A BOOKS</u>

1   LEVY, EUGENE. <u>James Weldon Johnson: Black Leader, Black Voice</u>.
Negro American Biographies and Autobiographies Series, edited by John Hope Franklin. Chicago and London: University
of Chicago Press, 380 pp.
Complete and thorough biography of Johnson. The James
Weldon Johnson Collection of Negro Arts and Letters as well
as Johnson's published works were used extensively. While
his various careers are recorded and discussed, more emphasis is placed on Johnson as a political and social figure
than on Johnson as author. As an N.A.A.C.P. leader, Johnson
was essentially a conservative, steady, middle-class influence although his activities as a recruiter and investigator
were forceful and courageous. As a writer, Johnson is seen
as less the innovator than some view him and more as a
skillful practitioner of art forms that have been introduced
by others. Major works and the critical reactions to them
are discussed at the appropriate moments in Johnson's life.
Insights into his works are derived from the collection of
Johnson's papers. Documentation is exceedingly thorough.
A checklist of Johnson's publications, including little-
known contributions to <u>Atlanta University Bulletin</u> and his
civil rights journalism for <u>The Crisis</u>, is appended along
with an extensive bibliography of secondary materials on
Johnson.

<u>1973 B SHORTER WRITINGS</u>

1   BAKER, HOUSTON A., Jr. "A Forgotten Prototype: <u>The Autobiogra-</u>
<u>phy of an Ex-Colored Man</u> and <u>Invisible Man</u>." <u>The Virginia</u>
<u>Quarterly Review</u>, 49 (Summer), [433]-49.

1973

Johnson's Autobiography is an important forerunner of
of Ralph Ellison's Invisible Man. Both protagonists are
nameless; both are restless men given to physical and
psychological flight; both are the products of miscegenation. Furthermore, both books owe a great debt to the folk
traditions of the trickster, the black badman, folk sermons
and oratory. Central to each novel is the "double vision"
of the protagonist who must view life both as a man and as
a "colored" man. Recognition of the ties between these
two novels can yield more insight than all of the commen-
taries written on Invisible Man. Reprinted 1974.B1.

2   SCHRAUFNAGEL, NOEL. "Before Native Son," in his From Apology
       to Protest: The Black American Novel. Deland, Florida:
       Everett Edwards, Inc., pp. 10-12.
          Johnson's Autobiography of an Ex-Coloured Man is not only
       a "panoramic view of Negro life," but an analytical book
       which examines "the color problem." More than any other
       author of his period Johnson analyzes racial prejudice and
       the influence it exerts on the Negro.

3   VAUTHIER, SIMONE. "The Interplay of Narrative Modes in James
       Weldon Johnson's The Autobiography of an Ex-Colored Man."
       Jahrbuch für Amerikastudien, 18 (1973), [173]-81.
          Johnson's Autobiography is a "deceptively simple book"
       which seems to be cast in the autobiographical mode--well
       established in Afro-American tradition by 1912--when it is
       actually presented in a picaresque mode. Johnson uses the
       interplay of these two modes to contradict the American
       dream--only by becoming a trickster can the protagonist be
       successful, yet at the end his success is nothing.

4   WAGNER, JEAN. "James Weldon Johnson," in his Black Poets of
       the United States. Translated by Kenneth Douglas. Original-
       ly published as Les Poètes Nègres des Etats-Unis (Paris:
       Librairie Istra, 1962). Urbana: University of Illinois
       Press, pp. 351-84.
          After a brief biographical sketch of Johnson, the chapter
       deals with his progress as a poet who moved from dialect
       verse to poems in standard English to stylistic experiments
       in language; at the same time Wagner points out how Johnson
       was torn between conformity and militance, entertainment
       and argument in the content and tone of his poems.

5   YOUNG, JAMES O. Black Writers of the Thirties. Baton Rouge:
       Louisiana State University Press, pp. x, 4, 29-33, 149-51,
       155, 156, 233, 237.

1973

In the 1930's many younger black leaders felt that Johnson was an outmoded "Uncle Tom." Young discusses Johnson's
ideas in Negro Americans, What Now? and his defense of his
own political position in Along This Way. Also summarizes
Johnson's contributions as a literary critic.

1974 A BOOKS - NONE

1974 B SHORTER WRITINGS

1   BAKER, HOUSTON A., Jr. "A Forgotten Prototype: The Autobiogra-
     phy of an Ex-Colored Man and Invisible Man," in his Singers
     of Daybreak: Studies in Black American Literature. Washing-
     ton, D. C.: Howard University Press, pp. 17-31.
     Reprint of 1973.B1.

2   BELL, BERNARD W. "Folk Art and the Harlem Renaissance," in
     his The Folk Roots of Contemporary Afro-American Poetry.
     Detroit: Broadside Press, pp. 27-31.
        Discusses Johnson's use of folk preaching in The Auto-
     biography of an Ex-Coloured Man and his comments on folk
     art in the Preface to The Book of American Negro Poetry.

3   BUNI, ANDREW. Robert L. Vann of the Pittsburgh Courier. Pitts-
     burgh: University of Pittsburgh Press, pp. 146-55, 160-61,
     260, 361.
        Detailed account of The Pittsburgh Courier campaign
     (1926-1929) to discredit Johnson and W. E. B. DuBois as
     N.A.A.C.P. leaders. Johnson's handling of funds was ques-
     tioned repeatedly, but controversy ended with a retraction
     by Robert Vann, the publisher of The Courier, in 1929.

4   BUTTERFIELD, STEPHEN. Black Autobiography in America. Am-
     herst, Massachusetts: University of Massachusetts Press,
     303 pp., passim.
        Discusses the common features of black American autobi-
     ographies with frequent citation of Along This Way as an
     example.

5   DAVIS, ARTHUR P. "James Weldon Johnson," in his From the Dark
     Tower: Afro-American Writers, 1900 to 1960. Washington,
     D.C.: Howard University Press, pp. 25-32.
        Capsule biography of Johnson, stressing his role as a
     pioneer who helped to prepare the way for the New Negro
     Renaissance. As a poet, Johnson showed considerable growth,
     beginning as a rather sentimental and derivative poet who
     sometimes wrote uninspired dialect poems and sometimes heavy-

handed protest, but going on to handle folk material in original and sophisticated ways and to produce really skill-ful ironic verse. Johnson's only novel, The Autobiography of an Ex-Coloured Man, has achieved considerable popularity over the years, and although Johnson did not originate the idea of passing, most novels that deal with the theme after 1912 owe something to his treatment. Briefly discusses Along This Way (perhaps "this success story is too success-ful"), Black Manhattan (a good source for study of the black theater), and The Book of American Negro Poetry.

6   FRANKLIN, JOHN HOPE. "The Harlem Renaissance," in his From Slavery to Freedom: A History of Negro Americans. Fourth edition. New York: Alfred A. Knopf, pp. 357, 375, 376, 379, 382, 384.
Discusses Johnson's importance to the Harlem Renaissance—as poet, novelist, editor, and critic.

7   JACKSON, BLYDEN and LOUIS D. RUBIN, Jr. "The Search for a Language, 1746-1923," in their Black Poetry in America: Two Essays in Historical Interpretation. Baton Rouge: Louisiana State University Press, pp. 1, 3-4, 14-15, 19-31, 35-36.
Describes Johnson's search for form, beginning with his use of literary English for some poems and dialect for others, and culminating in his employment of a stylized idiomatic medium for the sermons in God's Trombones. Style of Johnson's earlier and later poems is analyzed and con-trasted.

8   ROSENBLATT, ROGER. "The Autobiography of an Ex-Colored Man," in his Black Fiction. Cambridge, Massachusetts: Harvard University Press, pp. 173-84.
Johnson's novel is extraordinarily complex considering the time at which it was written. It has psychological complexity far beyond the work of most black authors of its period. The protagonist resolves his internal conflict by adapting to the dominant world around him; in doing so, he condemns himself for taking the easy way out and con-demns the society which has pushed him toward this choice.

9   ROSS, STEPHEN M. "Audience and Irony in Johnson's The Auto-biography of an Ex-Coloured Man." College Language Associ-ation Journal, 18 (December), 198-210.
Recent critics such as Marvin Garrett and Robert Fleming have been correct in reading Autobiography as an ironic work; however, the target of the irony is not the narrator him-self but the white world and its standards. The novel is

1974

thus "genuine tragedy, for Johnson never allows his irony to destroy compassion for the mulatto trapped by white values...." The reader must not apply to the narrator "the condemnation that Johnson rightly reserves for the psychological power of American whiteness."

10 WHITLOW, ROGER. "1890-1920: Developing Artistic Consciousness," in his Black American Literature. Totowa, New Jersey: Littlefield, Adams and Company, pp. 65-67; also pp. 54, 96, 185.

Johnson is the only contemporary of Charles W. Chesnutt who approaches him in ability. The Autobiography of an Ex-Colored Man goes beyond the "usually over-simplified 'tragic mulatto' theme" by adding psychological complexity to his protagonist, who is also the narrator.

1975 A BOOKS - NONE

1975 B SHORTER WRITINGS

1 GAYLE, ADDISON, Jr. "The White Man's Burden," in his The Way of the New World: The Black Novel in America. Garden City, New York: Doubleday, pp. 109-16.

Johnson "epitomizes conservative black thought in the period and symbolizes the old virtues based upon status and prestige." His only novel, The Autobiography of an Ex-Colored Man, is in keeping with his philosophy. He is too insistent on the superiority of the middle class over the black poor, and he spends too much time defending his system of values at the expense of dramatic action.

2 RUSH, THERESSA GUNNELS, CAROL FAIRBANKS MYERS, and ESTHER SPRING ARATA. "Johnson, James Weldon," in their Black American Writers Past and Present: A Biographical and Bibliographical Dictionary. Vol. II. Metuchen, New Jersey: The Scarecrow Press, pp. 429-34.

Brief biography of Johnson with a bibliography of his published books and a list of the anthologies and periodicals in which his shorter works appear. [A bibliography of secondary materials contains a number of errors and should be used with care.]

1976 A BOOKS - NONE

1976 B SHORTER WRITINGS

1   REDMOND, EUGENE B. Drumvoices: The Mission of Afro-American
    Poetry. Garden City, New York: Doubleday, 464 pp., passim.
        Treats Johnson briefly as writer of conventional and
    dialect verse, anthologist, novelist. God's Trombones is
    Johnson's masterpiece in the poetic genre, one of the best
    works of Afro-American poetry written to date.

2   SINGH, AMRITJIT. The Novels of the Harlem Renaissance. Uni-
    versity Park, Pennsylvania: Pennsylvania State University
    Press, 175 pp., passim.
        Johnson is discussed only as an influence on the black
    novelists who published during the years 1923-1933.

Arna Wendell Bontemps

Introduction

Arna Bontemps never achieved the widespread reputation that James Weldon Johnson did, but like Johnson he was a versatile author who wrote fiction, poetry, and history as well as an editor who did a great deal to bring other black writers to the attention of the American reading public. Bontemps came upon the literary scene as a young poet at a time when Johnson was at the height of his reputation, and he ended his career in the same position Johnson had held at his death: writer in residence at Fisk University in Nashville, Tennessee. However, partly because of the era in which he began to write, Bontemps always had to content himself with writing as an avocation while he worked as teacher and librarian to support his family.

Born October 13, 1902, in Alexandria, Louisiana, Bontemps grew up in Los Angeles and attended San Fernando Academy and Pacific Union College. From 1924, when he began to teach at the Harlem Academy in New York, until 1938, when he resigned his job at the Shiloh Academy in Chicago to take a Rosenwald Fellowship, Bontemps taught school. After the Rosenwald grant, which financed his travel in the Caribbean, Bontemps went to work in Chicago for the Illinois Writers' Project, a division of the Works Progress Administration. In 1943 he received his master's degree in library science from the University of Chicago and became Librarian at Fisk University, a position he held for the next twenty years. In the late 1960's Bontemps began to win tardy recognition for his achievements, and he was invited to the University of Illinois Chicago Circle Campus, where he taught for several years, and then to Yale University, where he was a visiting professor and the curator of the James Weldon Johnson Memorial Collection. From 1971 until his death in 1973 he was back at Fisk as writer in residence.

In the variety of projects he undertook, Bontemps exceeds even the impressive breadth of Johnson's literary interests. Beginning as a prize-winning poet—in 1926 and 1927 he won the Opportunity Alexander Pushkin Prize twice and The Crisis Poetry Prize once—he soon moved on to the short story and the novel. In 1931 his first novel God Sends Sunday was published, and in 1932 he won the Opportunity Short Story Prize for "A Summer Tragedy," still frequently reprinted in anthologies. The same year marked his entry into the juvenile field when he

co-authored a children's book, Popo and Fifina, with his friend Langston Hughes. Over the years he continued to write children's books,
eventually authoring and editing fifteen works for children and ado-
lescents, most of them books with a special appeal and inspiration for
minority children. He later collaborated again with Hughes on two
collections, The Poetry of the Negro (1949) and The Book of Negro
Folklore (1958). During the latter part of the 1930's Bontemps concentrated on carefully researched historical fiction, Black Thunder
(1936) and Drums at Dusk (1939), and on his first independently written children's books, You Can't Pet a Possum (1934) and Sad-Faced Boy
(1937).

The 1940's brought projects which differed from any Bontemps had
previously attempted. They ranged from a collaboration with musician
W. C. Handy on the latter's autobiography and an anthology of poetry
for young readers (Golden Slippers, 1941) to a historical book on
black migrations in America (They Seek a City, 1945) with Jack Conroy,
a fellow worker from the Illinois Writers' Project. Bontemps and Conroy also collaborated on three children's books during the 1940's and
1950's. A final historical book of the decade was The Story of the
Negro (1948).

As author, editor, and historian, Bontemps remained a prolific
and multifaceted writer. Having been a commercial failure as a novelist in the 1930's, he published no more novels although a collection
of short stories, The Old South, came out in 1973. Biographies of
George Washington Carver, Frederick Douglass, and Booker T. Washington,
and other inspirational books such as Famous Negro Athletes (1964)
were written for juveniles, but Bontemps also published a number of
books aimed at adults and even at the scholarly reader. By writing
100 Years of Negro Freedom (1961) and editing Great Slave Narratives
(1969) and The Harlem Renaissance Remembered (1972), he firmly established his credentials as a serious historian. With Jack Conroy he
expanded their 1945 book They Seek a City, publishing it as Anyplace
But Here (1966); he also brought up to date the poetry anthology done
with Hughes and republished it in 1970. Bontemps came back to poetry
with the publication of Personals (1964) in England, his only volume
of verse in spite of his early publication in that genre.

Bontemps died of a heart attack June 4, 1973, in his home in Nashville. During his last few years, honorary doctorates from Morgan
State College in Baltimore and Berea College in Kentucky, an appoint-
ment as honorary consultant to the Library of Congress, and visiting
professorships at leading universities had at least partially redeemed
the bright promise of the 1920's and 1930's.

The reception accorded Bontemps' early poetry was good, especially
among black critics. And his winning the Opportunity and Crisis prizes
did not go unnoticed in the literary world at large, for several of the
reviews of God Sends Sunday (1931) mention that Bontemps was a recog-
nized poet. However, Bontemps' first attempt at fiction disappointed

him. God Sends Sunday grew out of an earlier autobiographical novel
"about a sensitive black boy in a nostalgic setting," a work for which
Bontemps could not find a publisher. Turned down by three different
editors, Bontemps took their suggestions, developed a minor character
from that novel into Little Augie, and built his first published novel
around him.[1] Although the book did not attract a great deal of attention, the response of white reviewers showed that the editors' sugges-
tion had been useful. The anonymous reviewers of the New York Times
Book Review (1931.B1) and the Boston Evening Transcript (1931.B2) read
the novel in the spirit of the Harlem Renaissance, praising Bontemps
for his illustration of his race's "light-heartedness" and "emotion"
and--significantly--comparing the novel to a minstrel show. Black
critics Sterling Brown and W. E. B. DuBois had other responses to the
same features of the novel. Writing for Opportunity, Brown said that
the novel was flawed by melodramatic sections although on the whole he
thought that the character of Augie redeemed the book (1931.B6).
DuBois, who had bitterly attacked Claude McKay for his Home to Harlem
(1928), was not so kind and viewed God Sends Sunday as very similar to
McKay's book: "sordid," "depressing," and immoral (1931.B7). Of the
various reviews, perhaps the most illuminating is Gwendolyn Bennett's
in the New York Herald Tribune; Bennett seemed to understand the novel
better than most other critics of either race and concludes by calling
Bontemps "one of the important writers of his race" (1931.B5).

No such controversy surrounded the publication of Bontemps' first
two juvenile books. Popo and Fifina, published the year after God
Sends Sunday, was praised by reviewers as a model travel book
(1932.B2) and Bontemps and Hughes were praised for writing a book
that would appeal to both races. You Can't Pet a Possum (1934) was
greeted with similar approval. By the time he published his third
juvenile, Sad-Faced Boy (1937), Bontemps was well on his way to becoming a leading children's writer.

Meanwhile, his ambitious historical novel Black Thunder (1936)
was being reviewed well but selling poorly. In spite of the fact
that it was anything but flattering to whites, the reviewers for the
New York Times Book Review, New Republic, The Saturday Review of Literature, and the New York Herald Tribune all liked the novel and
praised Bontemps' characterization of Gabriel and his vivid recreation
of history. This time the black press agreed, with Sterling Brown
calling the book a "fine American historical novel" in Opportunity
(1936.B3) and later, in his book The Negro in American Fiction
(1937.B5), suggesting that Bontemps had filled a void in American
literature with his second novel. Benjamin Brawley, in The Negro
Genius (1937.B4) asked "if in the whole range of Negro fiction there
is a book to equal this in quality." But Bontemps, with his growing
family, was more influenced by the commercial failure of the book
than by the critical acclaim. In an introduction to the 1968 edition
of the novel, he recalled that his advance on the book was just enough
to pay his family's way to Chicago from California, where he had written the book while his family of five lived with his parents. The

book never earned more than its advance; Bontemps said that even as
he wrote the novel he had begun "to suspect that it was fruitless for
a Negro in the United States to address serious writing to my generation, and I began to consider the alternative of trying to reach young
readers not yet hardened or grown insensitive to man's inhumanity to
man...."[2]

Nevertheless, while pursuing his career as a children's writer,
Bontemps had a last try at writing fiction for adults. Drums at Dusk
(1939), the fruit of his first Rosenwald fellowship, was more widely
reviewed than either of his earlier novels. Opinion as to the quality
of Bontemps' third novel was mixed: while the reviewer for the New
Yorker felt that it was a sensational, melodramatic book (1939.B2),
and Rose Feld, writing for the New York Herald Tribune supplement
Books, thought characterization was weak and the plot too romantic
(1939.B6), more reviews praised the book than condemned it. C. D.
Abbott, of The Saturday Review of Literature, wrote that characterization was one of the book's strong points (1939.B1), and Margaret
Wallace said in the New York Times Book Review that Bontemps had
treated potentially sensational material in a restrained and artistic
manner, and that her sole criticism was that the book was so brief
and succinct (1939.B10). The widespread disagreement suggests that
it may have been difficult for critics to be objective about Drums at
Dusk, with its triumph of a black hero over a white ruling class that
is depicted satirically. At the same time he was receiving a mixed
response for his "adult" novel, however, Bontemps was being praised
for his juvenile writings. An article by Ione Rider in The Horn Book
Magazine concludes: "Whatever is yet to come from his pen we await
with anticipation, confident that it will be poetically conceived,
and written with distinction" (1939.B9).

In 1941, when Bontemps helped W. C. Handy to write his autobiography, the book received more attention than any other work he had yet
published, but most reviewers ignored Bontemps' contribution. Ex-
ceptions were Clifton Fadiman, who speculated in the New Yorker about
Bontemps' influences (1941.B10), and Charles Edward Smith, who mentioned in The Saturday Review of Literature that Handy had been aided
by "the distinguished Negro writer" Arna Bontemps (1941.B16). Also
published in 1941, Golden Slippers, his anthology of Afro-American
poetry for young people, was praised although the anonymous reviewer
for The Booklist wrote somewhat patronizingly of "the simple child-
like spirit of the Negro people" which the poems embodied (1941.B8).

In 1945 Bontemps and Jack Conroy's W.P.A. project resulted in the
publication of They Seek a City. Perhaps the era that welcomed Richard
Wright's Native Son (1940) and Black Boy (1945) was ready for a factual
book on black migrations, for nearly all reviews compliment its live-
liness, accuracy, and avoidance of special pleading and "sociological
cliches." Meanwhile, the two men continued the collaboration on
juveniles that had begun auspiciously with The Fast Sooner Hound
(1942), producing Slappy Hooper in 1946 and Sam Patch in 1951, all of
which were well received by library and school publications.

Introduction — Arna Wendell Bontemps

But the most notable work Bontemps produced during the 1940's was his far-ranging history The Story of the Negro (1948). Intended for young readers like so much of his work from the period, the book was reviewed on those terms by a variety of publications, but often with the note that adults could read the work with pleasure and would profit by the experience. Typical was the review by Henrietta Buckmaster in the Christian Science Monitor, which praised the comprehensiveness of the "painful but proud" history of the Negro from the ancient Egyptian era to the present and recommended it to children and adults (1948.B9). The Poetry of the Negro, co-edited with Langston Hughes and published the next year, was also praised by reviewers although nearly all of them criticized the absence of spirituals, and Jean Starr Untermeyer noted that there was much dross in the volume, mostly in the section of poetry written by whites about Negroes (1949.B10).

Throughout the fifties, Bontemps favored his career as a writer for children and teenagers, collecting good reviews and the Jane Addams Book Award for The Story of the Negro. Only toward the end of that decade and in the beginning of the 1960's did he return to earlier ambitions of writing and editing serious books for the adult market. When he and Langston Hughes published The Book of Negro Folklore (1958), it was accepted as a remarkable collection, in spite of the fact that neither of the editors was really a folklorist. Perhaps encouraged by this reaction, Bontemps offered adults a history (100 Years of Negro Freedom, 1961), an anthology (American Negro Poetry, 1963), and a collection of his verse (Personals, 1964). Curiously, in spite of his limited reception as a novelist, Bontemps was praised for using his skill as a novelist to bring history to life in 100 Years. The poetry books did not fare as well: American Negro Poetry disappointed most reviewers who did not look upon it with kindly condescension; only a few, such as Stephen Stepanchev of the New York Herald Tribune Books (1963.B6), really liked the anthology. Personals, published in a small edition by Paul Breman of London, went unnoticed by the American press.

Perhaps the two greatest achievements of Bontemps' last ten years were Great Slave Narratives (1969) and The Harlem Renaissance Remembered (1972). Each in its own way was seen by critics as an important contribution to the study of black culture although some complained that the introduction to the slave narratives could have been more analytical and some that The Harlem Renaissance was an uneven book, redeemed by Bontemps' introductory essay and a few of the other pieces.

Other than reviews, Bontemps has received scant critical attention, much of which does little more than suggest fruitful approaches for future critics. Benjamin Brawley's comments on Bontemps in The Negro Genius (1937.B4), although brief, are perceptive and helpful. The same might be said of Sterling Brown's short discussions of Bontemps the poet and Bontemps the novelist in his Negro Poetry and Drama (1937.B6) and The Negro in American Fiction (1937.B5). Ione Rider Morrison's "Arna Bontemps" in The Horn Book Magazine (1939.B9) is a helpful introduction to Bontemps as a children's writer.

Introduction — Arna Wendell Bontemps

The two best known literary histories of the black novel Hugh M. Gloster's Negro Voices in American Fiction (1948.B11) and Robert A. Bone's The Negro Novel in America (1965.B6) are both disappointing in their consideration of Bontemps. Gloster merely classifies Bontemps' novels as products of their respective eras, God Sends Sunday being viewed as a late product of the Harlem Renaissance and the two historical novels (though successful enough to encourage future historical novels on black themes) as products of the militant 1930's. Bone's opinions differ little from Gloster's except for his provocative though very brief treatment of Black Thunder. In less than two pages, Bone treats the historical backgrounds, narrative method, characterization, and symbolism in that novel, thus pointing out several areas which merit further analysis.

More recently, several really perceptive discussions of Bontemps have appeared. Dorothy Weil's "Folklore Motifs in Arna Bontemps' Black Thunder" (1971.B15) follows up a brief remark in Bone's study and illuminates one significant facet of the novel. Mary Gaver in "Realism and Children's Books" (1967.B6) opens interesting possibilities for the study of Bontemps' juveniles. Finally, Arthur P. Davis provides a brilliant overview of Bontemps as poet, novelist, and children's writer in his recent From The Dark Tower (1974.B5). However, one who examines the materials that have been written on Bontemps can only conclude that there is still much to be done, both in biography and in criticism of his varied literary works.

Some helpful starting points for such study are two articles written by Bontemps himself, "Sad-Faced Author"[3] and "The Lonesome Boy Theme."[4] Another basic resource is the interview with John O'Brien (1973.B17) in which Bontemps sheds light on several of his works. Finally, a note appended to Jack Conroy's recent reminiscence on his relationship with Bontemps (1976.B1) states that notes which Bontemps had made for his autobiography are being used by his son Alexander to write a biography.

Like the rise in his personal fortunes, Bontemps' literary reputation may be late in catching up with his achievement, but there are signs that the new interest will lead to greater appreciation of a complex and talented author.

NOTES

[1]Arna Bontemps, "The Awakening: A Memoir" in his The Harlem Renaissance Remembered (New York: Dodd, Mead and Company, 1972) pp. 25-26.

[2]Arna Bontemps, "Introduction" to his Black Thunder (Boston: Beacon Press, 1968), p. x.

[3]Arna Bontemps, "Sad-Faced Author," The Horn Book Magazine, 15 (January-February 1939), 7-12.

[4]Arna Bontemps, "The Lonesome Boy Theme," The Horn Book Magazine, 42 (December 1966), pp. 672-680.

Writings about
Arna Wendell Bontemps, 1926-1976

<u>1926 A BOOKS - NONE</u>

<u>1926 B SHORTER WRITINGS</u>

  1   ANON. "Our Prize Winners and What They Say of Themselves:
       Arna Bontemps." <u>Opportunity</u>, 4 (June), 188.
         Bontemps responds to interview questions by briefly
      summarizing his life and education, 1902 to 1926.

  2   ANON. "Krigwa: <u>Crisis</u> Prizes in Literature and Art, 1926."
       <u>The Crisis</u>, 33 (December), 70-71.
         Announces judges and prize winners of 1926 literary con-
      test. Bontemps took first prize in poetry with "A Nocturne
      at Bethesda."

<u>1927 A BOOKS - NONE</u>

<u>1927 B SHORTER WRITINGS</u>

  1   ANON. "Poetry and Painting." <u>The Crisis</u>, 34 (April), 48.
         Picture of Bontemps, a 12-line poem "Tree," and a brief
      note on him, including an autobiographical statement.

  2   ANON. "The Contest Spotlight: Arna Bontemps." <u>Opportunity</u>,
       5 (July), 204.
         Bontemps again responds to request for information, this
      time by mentioning his marriage and birth of his first child
      as additional biographical facts.

<u>1931 A BOOKS - NONE</u>

<u>1931 B SHORTER WRITINGS</u>

  1   ANON. "A Negro Jockey." <u>New York Times Book Review</u> (15 March),
       pp. 7, 18.

1931

Reviews God Sends Sunday. Bontemps is a young Negro from Louisiana who has already established a reputation as a poet. Now he has produced a novel with the vivid color of a minstrel show. Little Augie, the jockey, is a lively and sparkling, almost Byronic figure in his youth; as an old man he lives on his memories of glorious clothes and wild sprees. Bontemps has captured "the light-heartedness and the soft melancholy" of his race in a most artistic portrait.

2   ANON. Review of God Sends Sunday. Boston Evening Transcript (8 April), Part Three, p. 2.
Summarizes plot then notes "Mr. Bontemps deserves to be encouraged, for although this first book is less narrative than descriptive and has no great significance, it is presented with a becoming modesty and bears considerable promise, especially in its authentic rendering of negro language and emotion."

*3   ANON. Review of God Sends Sunday. Springfield Republican (12 April), p. 7E.
Listed in Book Review Digest.

4   ANON. "A Jockey of the 'Nineties." The Saturday Review of Literature, 7 (2 May), 801.
God Sends Sunday marks Bontemps' transition from poet to novelist, and he succeeds well with his depiction of Little Augie, a black jockey who spends his winnings on fancy clothes and fancy women. "Little Augie's sordid story is one told with economy and power."

5   BENNETT, GWENDOLYN B. "A Poet's Novel." New York Herald Tribune Books (22 March), p. 16.
Bontemps first attracted attention as a poet, and there is much poetry in God Sends Sunday, the beautifully written character study of a black jockey. "The author fashions the Little Augie of his heydey with good-natured indulgence and touches the old man with restrained pity that never becomes maudlin." He wisely emphasizes the art of the novel and avoids the pitfall of propaganda. "One cannot read this book without realizing that Arna Bontemps has taken his place as one of the important writers of his race."

6   BROWN, STERLING A. Review of God Sends Sunday. Opportunity, 9 (June), 188.
While Bontemps' first novel is too melodramatic in places and some of the characters seem flat, "the merits of the book are those of the folk ballads. The movement is swift and direct, the telling simple and interesting." And Augie rises above the melodrama to become a truly memorable folk character.

Writings about Arna Wendell Bontemps, 1926-1976

7   DuBOIS, W. E. B. Review of God Sends Sunday. The Crisis, 38
     (September), 304.
         Bontemps' first novel is a sordid work, roughly compara-
     ble to Carl Van Vechten's Nigger Heaven or Claude McKay's
     Home to Harlem. No ray of hope sheds any light in the dark-
     ness of this depressing story of crime and immorality. It
     is disappointing that the nobility which pervades Bontemps'
     best poetry is nowhere evident in this entire work.

*8   DUNBAR-NELSON, ALICE. "Book Chat." Norfolk Journal and Guide
     (16 May), n.p.
         Review of God Sends Sunday. Cited in James O. Young's
     Black Writers of the Thirties (1973.B24).

*9   JONES, DEWEY R. "God Sends Sunday." Chicago Defender (8 Aug-
     ust), n.p.
         Cited in James O. Young's Black Writers of the Thirties
     (1973.B24).

*10 POSTON, T. R. "New Book." The Pittsburgh Courier (18 April),
     n. p.
         Review of God Sends Sunday. Cited in James O. Young's
     Black Writers of the Thirties (1973.B24).

1932 A BOOKS - NONE

1932 B SHORTER WRITINGS

1   ANON. Review of Popo and Fifina. The Booklist, 29 (December),
     [118].
         A sincerely written book about the black people of Haiti,
     it "will interest children of fourth and fifth grades."

2   EATON, ANNE T. Review of Popo and Fifina. New York Times Book
     Review (23 October), pp. 13, 16.
         This model travel book presents not only facts but a real
     sense of what Haiti must be like for Haitians. It "tempts
     us to wish that all our travel books for children might be
     written by poets."

3   MAURY, JEAN WEST. "Books of the Season for Children." Boston
     Evening Transcript, Book Section (5 November), p. 2.
         Summarizes plot of Popo and Fifina and then remarks that
     "children white and black will enjoy reading about Popo and
     his older sister...and following them on their small adven-
     tures." Briefly sketches literary backgrounds of co-authors
     Bontemps and Langston Hughes.

Writings about Arna Wendell Bontemps, 1926-1976

1933

1933 A BOOKS - NONE

1933 B SHORTER WRITINGS

1   [CARTER, ELMER ANDERSON]. [Editor's note to "A Summer Tragedy"
     by Bontemps]. Opportunity, 11 (June), 174.
          Announces Bontemps' winning the Opportunity Literary
     Award for 1933 for "A Summer Tragedy," a short story printed
     in this issue of Opportunity. Notes that Bontemps previously
     won the Alexander Pushkin Prize for Poetry twice.

1934 A BOOKS - NONE

1934 B SHORTER WRITINGS

1   ANON. Review of You Can't Pet a Possum. New York Times Book
     Review (23 September), p. 9.
          Bontemps has told a charming story of a boy and his dog--
     their adventures in rural Alabama and in Birmingham--and has
     given it a distinctive flavor by using dialect that conveys
     the spirit of the South without being hard for a child to
     understand.

2   ANON. Review of You Can't Pet a Possum. The Horn Book Maga-
     zine, 10 (November), 359.
          "An amusing story of Shine Boy, a nine-year-old negro."

3   BENÉT, ROSEMARY CARR. "Children's Bookshop: Books for the
     Youngest." The Saturday Review of Literature, 11 (17 Novem-
     ber), 298.
          You Can't Pet a Possum, the story of Shine Boy, an eight-
     year-old black orphan, and his dog, employs dialect and humor
     in relating a series of adventures. A warm book for young
     readers.

4   MAURY, JEAN WEST. "Books of the Christmas Season for Children."
     Boston Evening Transcript (19 December), Part Three, p. 2.
          You Can't Pet a Possum is "a funny little story about
     real little black boys and some of their elders...." Very
     little plot but the characters are well created and the dia-
     lect is well written.

5   WATSON, KATHERINE. Review of You Can't Pet a Possum. Library
     Journal, 59 (1 November), 854.
          Bontemps tells the story of a nine-year-old Negro boy and
     his pet dog. The book is delightful from its plot to its
     presentation of dialect.

Writings about Arna Wendell Bontemps, 1926-1976

<u>1935 A BOOKS - NONE</u>

<u>1935 B SHORTER WRITINGS</u>

1   ANON. Review of <u>You Can't Pet a Possum</u>. <u>New York Herald Tri-</u>
<u>bune Books</u> (20 January), p. 7.
Bontemps' latest book is not only one of the best about
Negro children but one of the best children's books published
this year. As in <u>Popo and Fifina</u>, which he wrote with Langston Hughes, Bontemps' chief strength is in solid, believable
characterization. <u>You Can't Pet a Possum</u> is also noteworthy
for its range of moods--from sadness to humor.

<u>1936 A BOOKS - NONE</u>

<u>1936 B SHORTER WRITINGS</u>

1   ANON. Review of <u>Black Thunder</u>. <u>The Booklist</u>, 32 (April),
[232].
In this powerful novel of Virginia in 1800, Bontemps
treats the unsuccessful rebellion led by Gabriel, a slave
who attempted to take Richmond with an army of fellow
slaves. "Recreates the terror of the whites and the hopes
of the Negroes...."

2   BRICKELL, HERSCHEL. "The Negroes Rise," in his column "The
Literary Landscape." <u>Review of Reviews</u>, 93 (March), 19.
<u>Black Thunder</u> is one of the best novels yet written by
a black writer. Although he has little to work with in
solid historical facts, Bontemps writes well of antebellum
Virginia and the slaves who inhabited it.

3   BROWN, STERLING A. "The Literary Scene." <u>Opportunity</u>, 14
(July), 216.
Throughout <u>Black Thunder</u> it is apparent that the author
is a poet although here he has turned his hand to a historical novel. "<u>Black Thunder</u> stresses symbolic, imaginative
glimpses--poetic realism--rather than documentation." The
book is truthful as well as artistically told--"a fine American historical novel."

4   CLARK, EMILY. "Story of the 'Gabriel Insurrection.'" <u>New York</u>
<u>Herald Tribune Books</u> (2 February), p. 3.
Bontemps seems to stick to the historical facts in writing
about slavery and, in particular, about the Gabriel Insurrection in antebellum Virginia. His characterization of
Gabriel as a man with power and dignity and his use of realis-
tic dialect are strong points in <u>Black Thunder</u>, which shows
great power.

1936

5 D., J. Review of Black Thunder. The Saturday Review of Literature, 13 (15 February), 27.
       Arna Bontemps bases Black Thunder on history, but in most
   cases succeeds better than historians in making the past come
   to life. While portraits of some white characters seem to
   border on caricature, the depiction of the blacks, especially
   Gabriel, the leader of the revolt, is effective. (Bontemps
   is referred to as "she" throughout the review.)

6 GRUENING, MARTHA. Review of Black Thunder. The New Republic,
   86 (26 February), 91.
       Bontemps' novel is an imaginative and historically faith-
   ful account of the slave insurrection headed by Gabriel, a
   young Virginia slave, in the fall of 1800. He shows great
   skill in characterization, especially in that of Gabriel,
   whom he elevates to the stature of a tragic hero.

7 PETERSON, DOROTHY R. "Black Thunder." Challenge, 1 (June),
   45-46.
       Poetic descriptions and strong characterization are the
   most noteworthy characteristics of this powerful historical
   novel based on an actual rebellion near Richmond, Virginia,
   in 1800.

8 TOMPKINS, LUCY. "Slaves' Rebellion." New York Times Book Review (2 February), p. 7.
       Black Thunder is an historical novel, but also much more.
   By evoking Gabriel's response to the ideal of freedom, Bontemps has said something about mankind's potential in a uni-
   versal sense, and he has done so with a beautifully simple
   and precise style. By setting the novel in 1800, Bontemps
   has avoided modern prejudices that might have kept readers
   from hearing him out.

9 WRIGHT, RICHARD. "A Tale of Folk Courage." Partisan Review
   and Anvil, 3 (April), 31.
       Praises Bontemps for his revolutionary outlook and for
   the creation of his protagonist Gabriel, whom he endows "with
   a myth-like and deathless quality." "The only novel dealing
   forthrightly with the historical and revolutionary traditions
   of the Negro people."

1937 A BOOKS - NONE

1937 B SHORTER WRITINGS

1 ANON. Review of Sad-Faced Boy. The Horn Book Magazine, 13
   (May), 154.

"A fresh, unusual and amusing story" about three boys who visit Harlem, see the sights, and return to Alabama.

2   ANON. Review of Sad-Faced Boy. New York Herald Tribune Books (9 May), p. 10.
     "No one writes for children with a style more limpid than Arna Bontemps...." His books provide educational value as well as furnish amusement. This book, about Slumber Dozier and his two brothers, stays in the memory a long time after it is put down.

3   ANON. Review of Sad-Faced Boy. The Booklist, 33 (June), [313].
     This amusing story of three country boys who come to Harlem for the first time is intended for fourth and fifth grade readers.

4   BRAWLEY, BENJAMIN. "Arna Bontemps," in his The Negro Genius. New York: Dodd, Mead and Company, pp. 259-61.
     Although he began to write during the Harlem Renaissance, Bontemps should not really be identified with it--his work is much less influenced by fads. He has distinguished himself in poetry, but his novels are even better. God Sends Sunday has some unforgettable scenes, but a reader of Black Thunder "is led to ask if in the whole range of Negro fiction there is a book to equal this in quality."

5   BROWN, STERLING. "Southern Realism" and "Historical Fiction," in his The Negro in American Fiction. Washington, D.C.: Associates in Negro Folk Education, pp. 155-56, 197-98.
     Bontemps' first novel, God Sends Sunday (1931), is a realistic character study of a black jockey and an accurate picture of sporting life. Perhaps more significant, however, is his second novel, Black Thunder, in which he goes back in history to the Gabriel Prosser rebellion in 1800. Here he "bears witness to a staunch desire to be free--a fact of the Negro's past that most of the historical romancers have not cared to record." Besides evoking the spirit of freedom, he creates realistic and memorable characters.

6   _____. "Contemporary Negro Poetry," in his Negro Poetry and Drama. Washington, D.C.: Associates in Negro Folk Education, pp. 74-75.
     Bontemps is "a poet of distinction," whose work is "meditative" and "couched in fluent but subdued rhythms." Among his better poems are "Nocturne," "Nocturne at Bethesda," "Gethsemane," and "Golgotha Is a Mountain." He works effectively both in free verse and in the more established forms.

1937

7   BUELL, ELLEN LEWIS. Review of Sad-Faced Boy. New York Times
    Book Review (9 May), p. 12.
        With touches of humor and a real sense of the feeling
    of boyhood, Bontemps tells the story of three brothers who
    leave their native Alabama to visit their Uncle Jasper in
    Harlem. After adventures on the subway and among the Eighth
    Avenue pushcarts, they get homesick and return to the rural
    South. A good, mellow book for children.

8   LEE, ULYSSES. "The Boys Who'd Love to Laugh." Opportunity,
    15 (August), 247-48.
        In the vast wilderness of children's literature dealing
    with Negro childhood, Bontemps' Sad-Faced Boy is a welcome
    oasis. Writing sensitively and poetically Bontemps captures
    the wonder of country Alabama boys who see New York for the
    first time. He also shows great skill in conveying the
    exact flavor of Negro speech without lapsing into unintel-
    ligible dialect. While the book is not perfect--it could
    be more fully developed--Bontemps has shown just how much
    is possible, working in a field that has produced little
    up to now.

9   MACK, ELSIE M. "Stories of the Season for Young Readers."
    Boston Evening Transcript (8 May), Part Six, p. 4.
        Summary of plot of Sad-Faced Boy. "The story is straight-
    forward and realistic, the style simple and direct with in-
    cidents treated without caricature and well suited to child-
    ren's interests."

10 REELY, MARY KATHARINE. Review of Sad-Faced Boy. Wisconsin
    Library Bulletin, 33 (July), 132.
        "Sensitive humor and faithful characterizations" mark
    this book about three Alabama boys in New York. "The chap-
    ter on the library should not be missed by any children's
    librarian."

11 SPINGARN, ARTHUR B. "Books by Negro Authors in 1936." The
    Crisis, 44 (February), 47.
        Black Thunder, "written in beautiful poetic prose," is
    "the best historical novel written by an American Negro" in
    spite of the fact that it falls off somewhat in the last
    half.

1939 A BOOKS - NONE

1939

1   ABBOTT, C. D. "Black Thunder." The Saturday Review of Literature, 20 (13 May), 12.
    Characterization is the strong point in Drums at Dusk, an historical novel of black revolution in Santo Domingo, whether Bontemps is ironically cutting down the island's self-satisfied aristocrats, sympathetically representing the planters who had humanitarian impulses, or depicting the black hero Toussaint. He has told a powerful and valuable story, a major addition to Negro literature. [The reviewer seems unaware that the title of his review is the same as the title of Bontemps' earlier novel.]

2   ANON. Review of Drums at Dusk. New Yorker, 15 (6 May), 75.
    Unfortunately, Bontemps employs melodrama and sensationalism to tell the story of the 18th-century slave rebellion in Haiti.

3   ANON. "Drums at Dusk." Springfield Sunday Union and Republican (21 May), p. 7E.
    Summary of plot. The action is seen from the point of view of Diron Desautels, a Frenchman who sympathizes with the blacks. "About the only fault one can find with 'Drums at Dusk' is that it should have been longer.... With more space [Bontemps] might have developed his background and his characters more fully." The characters are somewhat vague and events surrounding the rebellion will puzzle readers who don't know their history. More about Toussaint is needed. Nevertheless it is a "welcome addition to the field of historical fiction."

4   ANON. "New Books: A Reader's List." The New Republic, 99 (24 May), 84.
    Brief mention of Drums at Dusk. Bontemps handles this novel of Toussaint L'Ouverture's Haitian revolt with considerable skill. Plot and characterization mesh nicely.

5   ANON. Review of Drums at Dusk. Pratt Institute Quarterly Booklist, Series 5, no. 111 (Autumn), p. 27.
    A "realistic picture of the Haitian slave revolt of 1791."

6   FELD, ROSE C. Review of Drums at Dusk. New York Herald Tribune Books (7 May), p. 16.
    Characterization is a weak point in this historical novel about the Haitian revolution of Toussaint L'Ouverture. Even Toussaint seems an unlikely figure to become a leader. The

1939

style is overly romantic and sometimes downright careless.
The strongest parts of the novel are in the scenes of rev-
elry just before the uprising, which depict the decadence
of the aristocracy well, and in the savage scenes taken from
the revolution itself.

7   LOGAN, RAYFORD W. "The Drums Still Beat." Opportunity, 17
     (July), 218-19.
          Bontemps has had to face two great handicaps in writing
     Drums at Dusk--American distaste for inter-racial love af-
     fairs and the problems of how closely to follow history. In
     spite of these difficulties he has written a powerful novel
     which catches the spirit of the Haitian rebellion.

8   OWENS, OLGA. "West Indian Slaves: Rebellious Days in an Effete
     Caribbean with Santo Domingan Aristocrat as Hero." Boston
     Evening Transcript (6 May), Part Four, p. 1.
          Sees Diron Desautels, white French aristocrat, as hero
     of Drums at Dusk, Toussaint as relatively minor character.
     The novel "progresses in a series of brilliant scenes. This
     distinguished Negro poet writes with passion and with power."
     Poignant scenes such as a mass suicide of slaves give way
     to scenes of triumph after the rebellion in such a way that
     the white reader's sympathy stays with the slaves.

9   RIDER, IONE MORRISON. "Arna Bontemps." The Horn Book Magazine,
     15 (January), 13-19.
          Brief discussion of Bontemps' life and writing career to
     1939, with emphasis on his children's books. Popo and Fif-
     ina, You Can't Pet a Possum, and Sad-Faced Boy are summarized
     and discussed.

10   WALLACE, MARGARET. "A Tale of the Slave Revolt in Haiti." New
     York Times Book Review (7 May), p. 7.
          One of the few criticisms of Drums at Dusk is that there
     might be more of it. Bontemps succeeds in capturing a few
     days at the beginning of the slave rebellion of Toussaint
     L'Ouverture so well that the reviewer wishes he "might have
     planned something altogether larger in scale." But consid-
     ering the rather sensational material, Bontemps tells his
     story with admirable restraint and considerable art.

1941 A BOOKS - NONE

1941 B SHORTER WRITINGS

1   ANON. "Obstetrician of the Blues." Time, 38 (7 July),
     71-72.

Handy is not really the father of the blues so much as
a "good businessman" who managed to promote music based on
the blues. Father of the Blues, however, is "admirable"--
well written, warm, and straightforward; Handy's life story,
like his music, has more than personal significance.

2   ANON. Review of Father of the Blues. Christian Century, 58
    (9 July), 886.
        Whether or not the reader approves of the music he crea-
    ted, W. C. Handy has had an interesting life and the book
    achieves a genuine appeal.

3   ANON. Review of Father of the Blues by W. C. Handy. The Book-
    list, 38 (September), 10.
        Identifies Bontemps as editor. Handy tells the story of
    his life, from his childhood to his final success as a com-
    poser of "blues" music, in an appealing style.

4   ANON. Review of Father of the Blues. The Open Shelf (October),
    p. 18.
        Handy tells the story of his life and discusses the hard-
    ships of Negro musicians.

5   ANON. Review of Father of the Blues. The Catholic World, 154
    (November), 252-53.
        This autobiography of W. C. Handy is not only the story
    of one man's life, but a history of the blues. It is also
    the story of the injustices and terrorism practiced against
    Negroes in the South. "His is an interesting story and
    well told."

6   ANON. Review of Golden Slippers. The Open Shelf (December),
    p. 24.
        This anthology of Negro poetry contains "many old favo-
    rites."

7   ANON. Review of W. C. Handy's Father of the Blues. Pratt
    Institute Quarterly Booklist, Series 6, no. 6 (December),
    p. 5.
        Brief mention of Handy autobiography, stressing his im-
    portance to popular music.

8   ANON. Review of Golden Slippers. The Booklist, 38 (15 Decem-
    ber), 135.
        Bontemps' anthology of Negro poetry for young readers re-
    flects "the simple childlike spirit of the Negro people."
    The selections effectively range from melancholy to gaiety.

1941

9   BERLINER, MILTON. "'Blues' Composer Writes of His Life."
    Springfield Sunday Union and Republican (20 July), p. 6E.
    Handy's story "of his early life in Alabama and his tours
    with Mahara's Minstrels constitute a valuable contribution
    to the history of the American scene." His hardships, which
    are often reflected in his music, help to explain why some
    of his songs have "become part of living American folk music
    while other popular hits have died a very permanent death."

10 FADIMAN, CLIFTON. "Books." New Yorker, 17 (5 July), 54.
    Handy not only tells about his musical career, but, per-
    haps even more important, he tells how it was to grow up in
    Florence, Alabama, with a stern, puritanical father. The
    style is well done, either by Handy or his editor, Arna Bon-
    temps.

11 FERGUSON, OTIS. "If Beale Street Could Talk." The New Repub-
    lic, 105 (14 July), 60.
    In spite of the significance and even excitement inherent
    in the material, Handy's autobiography is rambling, unorgan-
    ized and sometimes dull. While it was apparently edited by
    someone else, it needed more complete rewriting.

12 IVY, JAMES W. "Anthology of Negro Poetry." The Crisis, 48
    (December), 395.
    Golden Slippers, a varied collection of poetry by Negro
    poets--some famous and some so new as to have little estab-
    lished reputation--will appeal to adults as well as children,
    though it is intended primarily for the latter. "These poems
    catch the...humor and the charming insouciance of Negro life."

13 REELY, MARY KATHARINE. Review of Father of the Blues. Wisconsin
    Library Bulletin, 37 (October), 155.
    The story of this significant colored composer "is told
    with humor and tolerance and the book is one to place beside
    the several fine autobiographies of negroes who rose as lead-
    ers in other fields."

14 REYNOLDS, HORACE. Review of Father of the Blues. Christian
    Science Monitor Magazine Section (23 August), p. 10.
    This readable book, especially in its first section which
    treats Handy's experiences on Beale Street, is a commentary
    on "American social history, American musical history, the
    annals of minstrelsy, the revelation of the processes of
    creation, the feelings of a race...."

15 ROSE, ERNESTINE. Review of Father of the Blues. Library Jour-
    nal, 66 (1 May), 399.

Father of the Blues is valuable not only for its biographical information about Handy but for the light it sheds
on music of his entire era. The style, while it does not
appear "literary," is notable for its smoothness and sensi-
tivity.

16 SMITH, CHARLES EDWARD. "Memphis Symphony." The Saturday Review
of Literature, 24 (19 July), 10.
        Handy was assisted in writing Father of the Blues by Arna
Bontemps, "the distinguished Negro writer." The result is
a simple but dignified autobiography which not only tells
the story of Handy's life but also presents a view of Negro
popular music and offers constant insights into the problems
the Negro faces in America.

17 STEVENS, H. AUSTIN. "The Jovial Autobiography of W. C. Handy."
New York Times Book Review (13 July), pp. 4, 8.
        "Told with his race's appreciation of laughter and its
acceptance of sadness, packed with facts on the development
of American native music, W. C. Handy's autobiography is a
warming, delightful story which should appeal to anyone"
who has ever come in contact with his songs.

18 STREATOR, GEORGE. "Two Autobiographies." Commonweal, 34
(29 August), 450-51.
        Bontemps allows Handy himself to come through in this
autobiographical book. Handy tells his story, comments on
the blues, relates how he was swindled out of most of the
profits made by his "Memphis Blues." Father of the Blues
is "courageous, entertaining and highly informative."

19 VAN VECHTEN, CARL. "W. C. Handy, Dean of Negro Composers."
New York Herald Tribune Books (6 July), p. 1.
        Handy's life story, in the tradition of black autobiogra-
phy, tells not only about his struggles and eventual success,
but also of the frustrations of being a Negro in America.
His criticism is restrained, but it makes its point. The
biggest value of the book, though, is what it tells about
the kind of music Handy popularized--the blues.

1942 A BOOKS - NONE

1942 B SHORTER WRITINGS

1 ANON. Review of The Fast Sooner Hound. The Booklist, 39
(1 November), 73.

1942

Bontemps and Jack Conroy capture the spirit of the American tall tale in this story of a fireman's dog that would "sooner run than eat."

2   ANON. Review of The Fast Sooner Hound. Commonweal, 37 (20 November), 117.
    "Fantastic yarn" about "a dog...who can outrun any train."

3   EATON, ANNE T. "Early Railroad Days." New York Times Book Review (15 November), p. 8.
    Bontemps and Conroy's humorous tall tale of a dog that outraces trains is nicely complemented by Virginia Burton's action-filled drawings.

4   HARRISON, WILLIAM. "Selections of Negro Poetry." Opportunity, 20 (January), 27.
    Bontemps, a poet and historical novelist, has now edited a valuable collection of Negro poetry, ranging from spirituals, work-songs, and blues, through the "household names" such as Paul Laurence Dunbar, William Stanley Braithwaite, Countee Cullen, Langston Hughes, and James Weldon Johnson, and ending with the newer poets who are just beginning to achieve reputations. Golden Slippers should be "in every public and private library in the land."

5   HILL, RUTH A. "1942 Books for the Younger Children: A Selection for Children Under Ten." Library Journal, 67 (15 October), 881-82.
    In The Fast Sooner Hound, Bontemps and Conroy have produced the most satisfying and delightful illustrated book this year for this age group.

6   JORDAN, ALICE M. Review of The Fast Sooner Hound. The Horn Book Magazine, 18 (November), 417, 419.
    This tall tale is the story of a dog that can outrun trains to accompany his master, a railroad fireman. Well-illustrated.

7   REELY, MARY KATHARINE. Review of The Fast Sooner Hound. Wisconsin Library Bulletin, 38 (December), 188.
    The authors combine "two themes of great appeal to children, dogs and railroad trains," producing a story that "may become one of the popular nonsense tales."

8   SNOW, MIRIAM B. Review of The Fast Sooner Hound. Library Journal, 67 (15 October), 954.
    This tall tale about a speedy dog that would "sooner run than eat" is an amusing contribution for children around ten years old.

9   W., K. S.   "Books."   New Yorker, 18 (12 December), 106.
    "A fine tall story" and a "good example of native Ameri-
    can humor" with appropriate illustrations by Virginia Lee
    Burton.

1943 A BOOKS - NONE

1943 B SHORTER WRITINGS

1   ANON.   Review of The Fast Sooner Hound.   New York Herald
    Tribune Books (17 January), p. 8.
    Men as well as boys should find this "folk" story amus-
    ing, mixing, as it does, railroads, a dog, and tall-tale
    humor.   The illustrations match the text in tone and excel-
    lence.

2   D., E. V.   "For Younger Readers: 'Fast Sooner Hound.'"   Spring-
    field Sunday Union and Republican (17 January), p. 7E.
    This book is "cleverly designed to delight both children
    and parents."   Four to eight year olds should be pleased by
    both story and illustrations, done by Virginia Lee Burton.

3   SPINGARN, ARTHUR B.   "Books by Negro Authors in 1942."   The
    Crisis, 50 (February), 45.
    The Fast Sooner Hound "will be sure to delight all young
    children."   Bontemps is described as a "well known novelist
    and poet," but no mention is made of co-author Conroy.

1945 A BOOKS - NONE

1945 B SHORTER WRITINGS

1   ANON.   Review of They Seek a City.   Kirkus Reviews, 13
    (1 April), 150.
    Tells the story of the various migrations and "crusades"
    of the American Negro through the lives of leaders of the
    race.

2   ANON.   Review of They Seek A City.   New Yorker, 21 (16 June),
    71-72.
    Bontemps and Conroy manage to avoid the pitfalls that
    mar most books about "the Negro problem": emotionalism and
    "sociological cliches."   Their work is intelligent, tolerant,
    and interesting.

*3 ANON.   Review of They Seek a City.   Book Week (17 June), p. 3.
    Listed in Book Review Digest.

1945

4   ANON. Review of They Seek a City. The Booklist, 41 (1 July),
     315-16.
          Sketches the history of the Negro migration during four
     main periods: the days of the underground railroad, the
     period after Emancipation, World War I and World War II.

5   ANON. Review of We Have Tomorrow. Kirkus Reviews, 13
     (15 July), 318.
          While this book could be better written, its purpose is
     a worthy one: to tell the stories of twelve young Negroes
     who have become successful in spite of the difficulties
     imposed by race.

*6   ANON. Review of They Seek a City. U.S. Quarterly Book List,
     1 (September), 36.
          Listed in Book Review Digest.

7   ANON. Review of We Have Tomorrow. The Booklist, 42 (15 Octo-
     ber), 60.
          Intended for high school students, this selection of
     twelve brief biographies of young successful Negroes should
     promote "more democratic attitudes" and help provide "voca-
     tional guidance for Negro boys and girls."

8   ANON. Review of We Have Tomorrow. The Saturday Review of
     Literature, 28 (10 November), 79.
          Short biographies of twelve successful contemporary
     Negroes who have integrated jobs that were formerly closed
     to Negroes. "Informal and readable."

*9   ANON. Review of We Have Tomorrow. Book Week (11 November),
     p. 5.
          Listed in Book Review Digest.

10   ANON. Review of They Seek a City. The Open Shelf (November-
     December), p. 21.
          The readable, exciting story of the movement north and
     west by American Negroes.

11   DABNEY, VIRGINIA. "Negro Migrations." New York Times Book
     Review (10 June), p. 4.
          While they are objective throughout most of They Seek A
     City, Bontemps and Conroy are sometimes guilty of overlarge
     generalizations, as when they say that there was nothing
     good about the antebellum South from the slave's point of
     view. However, the authors do not condemn the South alone
     but point out that migration to the North has often left the
     Negro mired in wretched slums. For the most part, "a sound
     and valuable book."

1945

12   FRAZIER, E. FRANKLIN. "To the North." The Nation, 161
      (20 October), 411.
             They Seek A City is a lively and informative account of
      the migration of Negroes from the rural South to the urban
      North. The individual stories of early pioneers before
      World War I are more interesting than the history of mass
      migration that began with that war, but the entire book is
      valuable.

13   IVY, JAMES. W. "Race and Empire." The Crisis, 52 (December),
      362-63.
             The major difference between They Seek A City and previ-
      ous histories of Negro migrations is the skillful use of
      biographies of the interesting individuals who helped to
      lead these movements. This technique adds life to the
      account.

14   JORDAN, ALICE M. Review of We Have Tomorrow. The Horn Book
      Magazine, 21 (September), 417.
             A frank appraisal of racial discrimination in the United
      States through the stories of a dozen black Americans who
      became successful in spite of barriers. Adults may profit
      by reading the book though it is intended for children.

15   LOGAN, RAYFORD. "Seeking 'Any Place But Here.'" New York
      Herald Tribune Weekly Book Review (10 June), p. 5.
             "Arna Bontemps and Jack Conroy have...written a most
      timely study of the Negro's successive flights from oppres-
      sion...." While They Seek A City is aimed at the popular
      market, the authors have researched their material thoroughly.
      One of the few criticisms that can be made of this valuable
      book is that so much space is given to Chicago at the ex-
      pense of other cities.

16   PARKER, CHARLES J. "Negro Migrations from the South."
      Opportunity, 23 (Fall), 224.
             Although in They Seek A City Bontemps and Conroy have
      written a vivid, lively book that really conveys the feel
      of the Negro migration so that it is as if the reader is
      living it himself, they have been "far too hazy" in treat-
      ing "the total social implications which make these facts
      meaningful to the whole body politic."

17   REELY, MARY KATHARINE. Review of They Seek A City. Wisconsin
      Library Bulletin, 41 (July), 80-81.
             Two authors who have been engaged in research on the
      negro migrations join forces to produce an "interesting
      and readable" book on a significant movement.

1945

18   REELY, MARY KATHARINE. Review of We Have Tomorrow. Wisconsin
      Library Bulletin, 41 (December), 129.
           These biographical sketches of young negroes who have
      been successful in opening up professions "are interesting
      in themselves and could be used with good effect with high
      school students."

19   STREATOR, GEORGE. Review of They Seek A City. Commonweal,
      42 (20 July), 337-38.
           Bontemps and Conroy bring forth much new historical
      material in this book and skillfully retell some old
      stories. They are at their best when they let the facts
      speak for themselves, as they usually do, but are less
      successful when they propagandize. Many forgotten Negro
      heroes are recalled, among them frontiersman Jim Beckworth,
      historian Carter Woodson, and newspaperwoman Ida Wells.
      A helpful book on the positive aspects of Negro culture.

20   WELTMAN, ELIENNE RUTH. "We Have Tomorrow." Springfield Daily
      Republican (22 September), p. 4.
           Lists a number of the twelve subjects of the biographi-
      cal sketches. "Some of these stories are interesting, but
      the book as a whole has an effect of monotony.... Each
      story is written in the same manner, beginning with the
      trials and tribulations of childhood and ending with the
      ultimate success of the individual. The characters seem
      almost too perfect...." While the idea of the book is
      praiseworthy, its execution is not uniformly good.

1946 A BOOKS - NONE

1946 B SHORTER WRITINGS

1   ALSTERLUND, B. "Arna Bontemps." Wilson Library Bulletin, 20
      (January), 332.
           Biographical sketch of Bontemps covering his life from
      1902 to 1945. A summary of his education, teaching, and
      writing with some personal glimpses of Bontemps the man.

2   ANON. Review of Slappy Hooper. Kirkus Reviews, 14 (15 July),
      324.
           Slappy Hooper is reminiscent of Paul Bunyan--a sign-
      painter whose signs are so realistic they are invariably
      taken for the real thing. A different and amusing story.

3   BUELL, ELLEN LEWIS. Review of Slappy Hooper. New York Times
      Book Review (8 December), p. 22.

This book is not as exciting as the authors' earlier
tall tale The Fast Sooner Hound, but it is a good humorous story nevertheless.

4   KING, MARTHA. "Biggest and Best Sign Painter in the Whole
     World." Chicago Sun Book Week, 5, no. 8 (15 December), 7.
          Summarizes the feats of the tall-tale sign painter and
     recommends Slappy Hooper highly. "You'll hear about Slappy
     anywhere you go in America--that is, if you travel the way
     the authors did, with an ear to the heartbeats and tall
     tales of America."

5   TUNIS, JOHN. Review of We Have Tomorrow. New York Times Book
     Review (11 November), p. 22.
          Bontemps tells the stories of twelve young Americans
     who succeeded in spite of the great obstacles placed in
     their way by racism. In doing so he implicitly offers
     some well-deserved criticism of American race relations.

1947 A BOOKS - NONE

1947 B SHORTER WRITINGS

1   ANON. Review of Slappy Hooper. The Booklist, 43 (15 January),
     157.
          While the authors attempt to recapture the tall-tale
     atmosphere of their The Fast Sooner Hound, the current
     book about a miraculously fast and realistic sign painter
     "lacks the zest" of the earlier work.

2   NOLTE, CLAIR. Review of Slappy Hooper. Library Journal, 72
     (1 January), 82.
          The story of a miraculous sign painter is an amusing
     tale for children from nine to eleven.

1948 A BOOKS - NONE

1948 B SHORTER WRITINGS

1   ANDREWS, SIRI. "The Bond of Books." The Horn Book Magazine,
     24 (November), 476.
          Notes that The Story of the Negro is one of the best
     books read for this article: dignified, serious, informa-
     tive, especially about the countries of Africa. A power-
     fully influential book.

1948

*2 ANON. Review of The Story of the Negro. Kirkus Reviews, 16
     (15 April), 195.
        Listed in Book Review Digest.

3   ANON. Review of The Story of the Negro. New York Herald
     Tribune Weekly Book Review (30 May), p. 6.
        A concise, factual, and beautifully written history of
     the Negro people from ancient times to the present: "of-
     fered to the teens, it is for anyone old enough to think
     and young enough to keep on thinking."

4   ANON. Review of The Story of the Negro. The Booklist, 44
     (1 June), 338.
        In this "concise and readable" history for young read-
     ers Bontemps discusses the black people of Africa, Europe,
     Haiti, and the United States. Biographical sketches of
     famous Negroes appear at appropriate points within the
     history. Especially valuable for its "early background
     material."

*5 ANON. Review of The Story of the Negro. Christian Science
     Monitor (14 October), p. 13.
        Unlocatable. Listed in Book Review Digest.

*6 ANON. Review of The Story of the Negro. Survey Graphic, 37
     (November), 483.
        Listed in Book Review Digest.

7   ANON. Review of The Poetry of the Negro. Kirkus Reviews, 16
     (15 November), 609.
        A timely collection of verse by and about the Negro.
     Competently edited.

8   BAKER, NINA BROWN. Review of The Story of the Negro. New
     York Times Book Review (20 June), p. 21.
        This comprehensive history of the Negro people is "the
     answer to a librarian's prayer," written by Arna Bontemps,
     who is himself a librarian at Fisk University. High school
     students and adults can profit from the book.

9   BUCKMASTER, HENRIETTA. "Proud History and Urgent Problem."
     Christian Science Monitor (1 July), p. 15.
        In The Story of the Negro Bontemps tells the "painful
     but proud" history of the Negro, dating back to ancient
     Egypt, in a short book that will be good reading for adults
     as well as children.

10 [DAVIS, MARY GOULD]. Review of The Story of the Negro. The
     Saturday Review of Literature, 31 (14 August), 36.

Writings about Arna Wendell Bontemps, 1926-1976

Without prejudice or special pleading Bontemps presents
a well-researched history in an effective style. He traces
the story of the race from the Egyptian civilization of
1700 B.C. to the present, emphasizing the lives of black
heroes as diverse as Aesop, Crispus Attucks, Phillis Wheatley, Booker T. Washington, and Dr. DuBois. Raymond Lufkin's
illustrations are beautiful and dignified.

11 GLOSTER, HUGH M. "Arna Bontemps," in the chapters "Fiction
of the Negro Renascence" and "The Depression Decade," in
his Negro Voices in American Fiction. Chapel Hill: University of North Carolina Press, pp. 172-73, 213-16.
Like Carl Van Vechten's Nigger Heaven, God Sends Sunday
emphasizes sex and the sporting life although Bontemps does
not set his novel in Harlem. God Sends Sunday is also
noteworthy for its avoidance of any militant stand on
race. In Black Thunder and Drums at Dusk, in contrast,
Bontemps portrays slaves who have "an obsessive love for
freedom." Both of these historical novels suggest that
the Negro's past may be an excellent source of material
for the novelist.

12 JOHNSON, SIDDIE JOE. Review of The Story of the Negro. Library
Journal, 73 (15 May), 825.
Although this history of the black race from ancient to
modern times is intended for young readers, even adults
will find it fascinating.

13 JORDAN, ALICE M. "Summer Booklist." The Horn Book Magazine,
24 (July), 280-82.
The Story of the Negro is restrained, dignified, moving,
clear, excellent in every way. A well-written, significant
book.

14 McDONALD, GERALD. Review of The Poetry of the Negro. Library
Journal, 73 (15 December), 1818.
This comprehensive collection of good poetry should
become the standard anthology of black poetry. Its arrange-
ment into American poets, Caribbean poets, and non-Negroes
writing about black people keeps it from appearing as uni-
fied as some anthologies on the subject.

15 MOORE, ANNE CARROLL. "The Three Owls' Notebook." The Horn
Book Magazine, 24 (July), 267.
Finds The Story of the Negro "the most absorbing presen-
tation of Negro history that I have ever read." Bontemps is
a notable writer of children's books.

1948

16   MORGAN, NANETTE V. Review of The Story of the Negro. San
     Francisco Chronicle, Children's Book Issue (14 November),
     p. 11.
         "The most complete history ever written" about the
     race, "it is a must for those who are friendly, and for
     those likewise who are supercilious. For the Negro him-
     self, it will contribute to his sense of dignity and worth."

17   OTTLEY, ROI. "Primer for White Folks." The Saturday Review
     of Literature, 31 (26 June), 14-15.
         Bontemps, chief librarian of Fisk University, has under-
     taken a major job--to convey the world-wide history of the
     Negro people to young black readers (or to white readers
     of any age). Bontemps starts with slavery in the earliest
     recorded times and treats a number of distinguished slaves
     through history: Aesop, the Roman dramatist Terence, Tous-
     saint L'Ouverture, Gabriel Prosser, Nat Turner, and Frederick
     Douglass. The Story of the Negro is strongest in dealing
     with the period up to the American Civil War. While there
     are some dead spots in the work, on balance it is a note-
     worthy achievement.

18   THOMPSON, ERA BELL. "Dramatic and true-to-life story of Negro."
     Chicago Sun Book Week (13 June), p. 8.
         The best history of the Negro people yet written, trac-
     ing them from the Egypt of 5000 B.C. to the present day.
     Although it is "authentic history," the book is as exciting
     and interesting as good fiction.

19   THOMPSON, ORILLA M. Review of The Story of the Negro. Wiscon-
     sin Library Bulletin, 44 (June), 130.
         This history of the negro in America is "the most
     interesting and concise work for the general reader on
     the subject that has appeared." Recommended for high school
     students and adults.

1949 A BOOKS - NONE

1949 B SHORTER WRITINGS

1   ANON. "Reprints, New Editions." New York Herald Tribune Week-
     ly Book Review (16 January), p. 17.
         The Poetry of the Negro, which includes Negro poets
     from the United States, Africa, and the Caribbean, plus
     white poets writing on the Negro, is the best collection
     of its kind to date.

1949

2   ANON. Review of <u>The Poetry of the Negro</u>. <u>New Yorker</u>, 24
     (29 January), <u>71-72</u>.
          The editors omit spirituals and folk songs from this
     anthology, but there are interesting selections, especially
     among the newer poets such as Gwendolyn Brooks. Generally
     the poetry is of about average quality.

*3   ANON. Review of <u>The Poetry of the Negro</u>. <u>Chicago Sun</u>
     (31 January), n. p.
          Unlocatable. Listed in <u>Book Review Digest</u>.

4   ANON. Review of <u>The Poetry of the Negro</u>. <u>The Booklist</u>, 45
     (15 February), <u>207</u>.
          This is a varied collection grouped under three headings:
     poems by American Negroes, tributary poems by non-Negroes,
     and poems from the Caribbean. Within the headings there
     is no organization.

5   ANON. Review of <u>The Poetry of the Negro</u>. <u>The Open Shelf</u>
     (March-April), p. 5.
          This anthology is "a fine expression of the Negro's own
     poetic ability...."

6   CREEKMORE, HUBERT. "Two Rewarding Volumes of Verse." <u>New
     York Times Book Review</u> (30 January), p. 19.
          <u>The Poetry of the Negro</u> is probably the most comprehen-
     sive anthology of its kind to date. Several poets such as
     Robert Hayden, Owen Dodson, Margaret Walker, and Gwendolyn
     Brooks, who do not appear in older collections, are repre-
     sented here. Unfortunately, no folk-songs are included;
     they would have strengthened the book and the tributary
     poems by whites could have been omitted. The book "can
     help the reader understand the Negro's emotions, longings
     and values."

7   FERRIL, THOMAS HORNSBY. Review of <u>The Poetry of the Negro</u>.
     San Francisco <u>Chronicle</u>, <u>This World</u> [magazine section]
     (13 February), p. 15.
          A large, important collection of 147 poets--black poets
     and whites who have written about Negroes. Unfortunately,
     the poetry of black music such as spirituals and blues has
     been arbitrarily omitted.

8   HUMPHRIES, ROLFE. "Negro Verse." <u>The Nation</u>, 168 (19 February),
     217.
          "In a collection of this scope there is bound to be more
     verse than poetry," and many of the poets represented in
     <u>The Poetry of the Negro</u> are disappointingly conventional.

1949

However, the excellence of the good poets redeems those who
are mediocre. Especially notable are some of the new, rela-
tively unknown poets such as Helene Johnson and M. Carl Hol-
man.

9   SPINGARN, ARTHUR B. "Books by Negro Authors in 1948." The
     Crisis, 56 (February), 45.
        Although Bontemps' The Story of the Negro is intended
     for young readers, it is "the best written, most interest-
     ing and accurate of any of the concise histories available
     to the general reader."

10   UNTERMEYER, JEAN STARR. Review of The Poetry of the Negro.
     The Saturday Review of Literature, 32 (19 March), 16.
        In spite of the fact that both Langston Hughes and Bon-
     temps are poets, this anthology of poetry by and about
     Negroes is not successful. Part of the problem is that it
     attempts two things at once--to collect poems on various
     topics by black poets and to collect "tributes" by white
     poets as various as Blake, Elizabeth Barrett Browning, Whit-
     man, Longfellow, and Sandburg. The editors would have done
     better to have limited themselves to poetry by black poets.
     Furthermore, any anthology of black poetry should include
     a sampling of the spirituals, whose poetry is superior to
     much of the contents of this book. There is much excellent
     poetry in the volume, however, especially the poems of James
     Weldon Johnson, "O Black and Unknown Bards" and "The Crea-
     tion."

1950 A BOOKS - NONE

1950 B SHORTER WRITINGS

1   FLEMING, G. JAMES and CHRISTIAN E. BURCKEL. "Bontemps, Arna
     Wendell," in Who's Who in Colored America. Yonkers-on-Hud-
     son, New York: Christian E. Burckel and Associates, p. 40.
        Biographical sketch and list of Bontemps' book-length
     publications to 1950.

1951 A BOOKS - NONE

1951 B SHORTER WRITINGS

1   A., M. P. Review of Chariot in the Sky. The Saturday Review
     of Literature, 34 (21 July), 47.
        Centering on the life of Caleb Willows, a former slave
     who goes to Fisk University shortly after the Civil War,

1951

Chariot in the Sky tells the story of Fisk and its Jubilee
Singers, originally founded as a fund-raising group for the
university. Not only did the singers save Fisk from bank-
ruptcy, but they helped to preserve the slave songs that
they performed. "Deserves thoughtful attention."

*2 ANON. Review of Sam Patch. Kirkus Reviews, 19 (15 January),
    24.
        Listed in Book Review Digest.

3   ANON. Listing of Sam Patch. The Bookmark, 10 (February), 110.
        Lists and notes that it is suitable for children under
    nine.

*4 ANON. Review of Chariot in the Sky. Kirkus Reviews, 19
    (1 March), 129.
        Listed in Book Review Digest.

5   ANON. Review of Sam Patch. The Booklist, 47 (15 March), 260.
        The story of a unique contest between Sam, a great jump-
    er, and Hurricane Harry, another tall-tale hero. The story
    is humorous and full of action but "lack[s] some of the
    flavor of the tall tale."

6   ANON. Review of Sam Patch. The Saturday Review of Literature,
    34 (21 April), 40-41.
        This "well-told American yarn" about a series of jumping
    contests between two frontier characters should be enjoyed
    by older children as well as the younger ones for whom it
    is intended. The drawings, like the story, are full of
    humor and action.

7   ANON. Review of Sam Patch. Wisconsin Library Bulletin, 47
    (May), 124.
        An appealing and "hilarious" tall tale which should de-
    light children from grades 4 to 6.

8   ANON. Review of Chariot in the Sky. The Booklist, 47 (15 May),
    332.
        Bontemps tells the story of the beginnings of Fisk Uni-
    versity and the Jubilee Singers through the story of Caleb
    Willows, a former slave. "Although it is not too engrossing,
    perhaps, as a narrative, the book pictures well the plight
    of the Negro during the war and reconstruction...."

9   ANON. Review of Sam Patch. Christian Science Monitor (2 June),
    p. 11.

1951

An especially good children's book of the tall tale
genre. There is a great deal of humor throughout.

10 ANON. Notice of Chariot in the Sky. The Bookmark, 10 (July),
233.
Recommended for "older boys and girls."

11 ANON. Review of Chariot in the Sky. The Crisis, 58 (August-
September), 469.
Bontemps' history of the Fisk Jubilee Singers, told
through the story of "Caleb Williams [sic]" is "an exciting
and informative story for young people."

*12 ANON. Review of Sam Patch. U.S. Quarterly Book Review, 7
(September), 245.
Listed in Book Review Digest.

13 BAKER, AUGUSTA. Review of Chariot in the Sky. Library Journal
76 (1 June), 970.
Through the story of Caleb Willows, Bontemps dramatizes
the early years of Fisk University, emphasizing the importance of the Jubilee Singers. Offering valuable insights
into black life during and immediately after slavery, it is
"an excellent book to use with other material on slavery,
Civil War, and the Reconstruction Period."

14 BAKER, NINA BROWN. "Where Freedom Rings." New York Times Book
Review (17 June), p. 24.
Bontemps, "a distinguished Negro scholar" tells the
story of the end of slavery, the founding of Fisk University,
and the origins of the Jubilee Singers. Chariot in the Sky
is "thoughtful" and "enlightening," a worthy addition to
Winston's "Land of the Free Series."

15 [BECHTEL, LOUISE S.] Review of Sam Patch. New York Herald
Tribune Book Review (13 May), p. 7.
Bontemps' name on the book guarantees that this newly
invented tall tale will be well written. It is a good,
exciting book for boys from nine to twelve.

16 B., E. L. "Jumping Sam." New York Times Book Review (25 Feb-
ruary), p. 30.
"Exaggeration and...dead-pan humor" mark this tall tale,
Sam Patch, about a fabulous young jumper who joins the cir-
cus and engages in a lengthy jumping contest with his rival,
Hurricane Harry.

17 BURKE, EVELYN PERKINS. Review of Chariot in the Sky. Music
Library Association Notes, 8 (September), 717-18.

1951

"With a smooth, moving style--lively, genuine, and
realistic--Dr. Bontemps has here presented to young people
one of the most memorable and heart-stirring stories since
Booker T. Washington's Up From Slavery." The book "inspires
the reader with a new appreciation for an important aspect
of the great American heritage--the culture of the Negro
race."

18   CROMIE, ROBERT. Review of Sam Patch. Chicago Sunday Tribune
       Magazine of Books (25 February), p. 11.
            Arna Bontemps and Jack Conroy, who earlier created the
       larger than life figures of Slappy Hooper the sign painter
       and "The Fast Sooner Hound," have produced "another charac-
       ter in the same delightful pattern." Sam Patch is a legend-
       ary jumper whose story is "a fine bit of modern folk-lore."

19   FARRELL, ALFRED. Review of Chariot in the Sky. The Midwest
       Journal, 4 (Winter), 153-54.
            Summarizes the plot and notes that Bontemps has had ex-
       perience with the historical novel before in Black Thunder
       and Drums at Dusk. Chariot is both an inspirational story
       and an effective attack on bigotry.

20   H., H. "Two More in 'Land of the Free' Series: 'Chariot in
       the Sky,' 'Watergate' Added." Springfield Sunday Republi-
       can (6 May), p. 26 A.
            Summarizes Chariot and assesses it as an "excellent
       addition" to the series. While the book is written pri-
       marily for young readers, adults will enjoy it as well.

21   LINDQUIST, JENNIE D. and SIRI M. ANDREWS. "Late Winter Book-
       list." The Horn Book Magazine, 27 (March), 100.
            Sam Patch, a western tall tale about a fabulous jumping
       boy, his rival Hurricane Harry, and the latter's performing
       bear Chucklehead, is appealing and should please children
       from seven up.

22   _____. "Early Fall Booklist." The Horn Book Magazine, 27
       (September), 333.
            Adults as well as children could benefit from Chariot
       in the Sky, which tells of the origins of Fisk University
       and the Jubilee Singers. Bontemps shows great skill in
       his treatment of conditions before and after the Civil War.

23   S[COGGIN], M[ARGARET] C. Review of Chariot in the Sky. New
       York Herald Tribune Book Review (13 May), p. 16.
            Summarizes plot and then notes, "This narrative offers
       fresh material, but seems to lack...zest and vitality...."

WRITINGS ABOUT ARNA WENDELL BONTEMPS, 1926-1976

1951

24   SNOW, MIRIAM B. Review of Sam Patch. Library Journal, 76
      (1 March), 415.
           An entertaining tall tale suitable for reading aloud
      to fourth and fifth grade children.

1953 A BOOKS - NONE

1953 B SHORTER WRITINGS

1   HUGHES, CARL MILTON. The Negro Novelist: A Discussion of the
     Writings of American Negro Novelists, 1940-1950. New York:
     The Citadel Press, pp. 37, 38, 39, 210, 221, 228, 244.
          Bontemps' novels of the thirties are briefly mentioned
     as possible influences on novelists of the forties, and his
     critical reviews of these later novelists are quoted.

1954 A BOOKS - NONE

1954 B SHORTER WRITINGS

*1   ANON. Review of The Story of George Washington Carver. San
      Francisco Chronicle (16 May), p. 16.
           Listed in Book Review Digest.

2   BUELL, ELLEN LEWIS. "Three Americans." New York Times Book
      Review (20 June), p. 16.
           Of these three biographies for readers 8 to 12 (George
      Washington Carver, General Custer, and Clara Barton in the
      Grosset and Dunlap Signature Series), Bontemps' biography
      of Carver "has the most enduring value." "A moving portrait,
      unsentimentalized, written with restraint and sensitivity."

3   KINKEAD, KATHARINE T. Review of George Washington Carver. New
      Yorker, 30 (27 November), 220.
           "A superior biography for children of from eight to
      twelve, written with simplicity and deep feeling...."

4   MORRISON, HARRIET. Review of George Washington Carver. Library
      Journal, 79 (1 May), 864.
           Told in a simple straightforward style, Bontemps' life
      of Carver should be an inspirational book for young black
      readers and an informative work for whites as well.

1955 A BOOKS - NONE

1955 B SHORTER WRITINGS

*1 ANON. Review of Lonesome Boy. Kirkus Reviews, 23 (1 March),
    170.
        Listed in Book Review Digest.

*2 ANON. Review of Lonesome Boy. San Francisco Chronicle
    (22 May), p. 21.
        Listed in Book Review Digest.

3   ANON. Review of Lonesome Boy. The Bookmark, 15 (November), 41.
        A poetic fantasy, "a fine, sensitive story of a New
    Orleans boy who loves music and is lonesome without his
    trumpet," the book is also beautifully illustrated.

4   BAKER, AUGUSTA. Review of Lonesome Boy. The Saturday Review,
    38 (19 March), 40.
        This story of Bubber, a young trumpet player, is a very
    unusual children's story. The boy is a great young musician
    but is warned by his grandfather, also a trumpet player, to
    be careful how and when he plays the horn. Finally Bubber
    learns this lesson for himself in a surrealistic party scene
    where "the Host might well have been the Devil himself."

5   B[ECHTEL], L[OUISE] S. Review of Lonesome Boy. New York
    Herald Tribune Book Review (7 August), p. 8.
        This "beautifully written short story" employs the folk
    tradition of a devil's ball to teach a lesson to its main
    character Bubber and to the reader. Topolski's pictures
    complement the story well.

6   B., E. L. "The Silver Trumpet." New York Times Book Review
    (1 May), p. 28.
        This story of Bubber, the young trumpeter who plays at
    the devil's ball "has something of the quality of legend"
    about it. Lonesome Boy can be read as a warning against
    losing one's self in a private world and ignoring other
    people.

7   DONLON, RAE EMERSON. Review of Lonesome Boy. Christian
    Science Monitor (10 March), p. 4.
        This story of Bubber, the young trumpet player, and the
    lesson he has to learn through experience is well told by
    Bontemps and beautifully illustrated by Feliks Topolski.

8   HAVILAND, VIRGINIA. Review of Lonesome Boy. The Horn Book
    Magazine, 31 (June), 194-95.

1955

Bontemps evokes the spirit of jazz with this story of
Bubber, the young trumpet player who plays--or dreams he
plays--at the devil's ball. Young readers or even adults
will have to interpret the story for themselves.

9 MATHES, MIRIAM SNOW. Review of Lonesome Boy. Library Journal,
80 (15 April), 1008.
This story of a young black boy who is obsessed with
the idea of becoming a great trumpet player is worthwhile,
but too subtle for most children. In poetic style Bontemps
attempts to convey the idea that "a horn can do nothing for
lonesomeness but make it hurt worse," a message that will
not be grasped by the average child.

1958 A BOOKS - NONE

1958 B SHORTER WRITINGS

*1 BONE, ROBERT A. "Aspects of the Racial Past," in his The Negro
Novel in America. New Haven and London: Yale University
Press.
See 1965.B6.

1959 A BOOKS - NONE

1959 B SHORTER WRITINGS

1 ANON. Review of The Book of Negro Folklore. The Bookmark,
18 (January), 91.
Hughes and Bontemps have compiled an "inclusive collection
by subject of the Negro contribution to American culture...."

2 ANON. Review of The Book of Negro Folklore. Wisconsin Library
Bulletin, 55 (January), 53.
Includes "a wide range of Negro folklore," as well as
literary pieces influenced by folklore.

3 ANON. Review of The Book of Negro Folklore. The Booklist,
55 (1 January), 230.
The collection offers samples of a wide range of Negro
folk materials--tales, ballads, sermons, blues, spirituals--
and stories and poems employing folk material. "A comprehensive collection."

*4 ANON. Review of The Book of Negro Folklore. San Francisco
Chronicle (4 January), p. 22.
Listed in Book Review Digest.

Writings about Arna Wendell Bontemps, 1926-1976

5   ANON. Review of Frederick Douglass: Slave-Fighter-Freeman.
    The Booklist, 55 (15 June), 575.
        This biography, which emphasizes Douglass' early life,
    is "well-written...easily read, perceptive." Intended for
    children in grades 5 to 8.

6   ANON. Review of Frederick Douglass. Wisconsin Library Bul-
    letin, 55 (July), 359.
        This biography of the famous Negro leader is both well
    written and inspiring, recommended for grades 5 to 7.

7   BAKER, AUGUSTA. Review of Frederick Douglass. Library Journal,
    84 (15 May), 1693.
        Bontemps succeeds in evoking the "excitement and dignity"
    of Douglass' life from his days in slavery to his career
    as abolitionist.

8   BOTKIN, B. A. "The Negro Folk Tradition in America." New York
    Herald Tribune Book Review (1 February), p. 3.
        Hughes and Bontemps interpret folklore broadly, "as a
    way of life and looking at life," a broad cultural approach.
    The Book of Negro Folklore thus runs from animal stories
    and tales of magic to Harlem slang and modern prose and
    poetry employing folklore. More commentary and notes by
    the editors would have made the book even more valuable
    for a serious student of folklore, however.

9   BUELL, ELLEN LEWIS. "Escape to Freedom." New York Times Book
    Review (21 June), p. 22.
        In Frederick Douglass, Bontemps deals mostly with Doug-
    lass' youth, since the material appeals to the age group
    (9 to 13) he is writing for. This is also the most drama-
    tic part of Douglass' life--his experiences in slavery and
    his escape to the North. While Bontemps summarizes Doug-
    lass' later career, he might have gone into more detail
    about the period following the Civil War. On the whole,
    an effective, moving biography.

10 FLYNN, JANE ANN. Review of Frederick Douglass. Social Edu-
    cation, 23 (November), 359.
        Douglass' motives and feelings are brought out clearly
    in this story of his early life for grades 5 to 9.

11 I., J. W. Review of The Book of Negro Folklore. The Crisis,
    66 (March), 181-82.
        "A remarkable and comprehensive collection of Negro folk
    literature," from animal stories to the blues. Bontemps'
    "genial commonsense" introduction is helpful in pointing
    out the uniqueness of Afro-American folklore.

1959

12   PARKER, JOHN W. "Negro Folklore: Segment of American Culture."
College Language Association Journal, 2 (March), 185-86.
      Langston Hughes and Bontemps include a wide range of
folklore from slavery times to the present in The Book of
Negro Folklore, which "sheds light upon the old and the
new, the fantastic and the factual, the humorous and the
sad."

13   REDDING, SAUNDERS. "Sunshine and Shadows." New York Times
Book Review (18 January), p. 5.
      While some collections of folklore are intended for
scholars and some for general readers, Langston Hughes and
Bontemps have produced a book that will appeal to both
classes. The Book of Negro Folklore is a large volume,
including sermons, spirituals, blues, ghost stories, slang
terms, but perhaps the most provocative section is the last,
in which the editors collect modern pieces of writing that
are dependent on folklore. These suggest that the current
Negro intellectual is digging into his cultural heritage and
realizing its value.

14   SMITH, WILLIAM RAYMOND. "To Make Us Love Our Country." The
New Republic, 140 (16 February), 19-20.
      Compares black folklore with Kentucky mountain folklore
(as collected in Marie Campbell's Tales from the Cloud
Walking Country) and finds that the two have much in common
and give hope of a united America. In The Book of Negro
Folklore, Langston Hughes and Bontemps "have edited one of
the best anthologies it has been my pleasure to see."

15   TAYLOR, MILLICENT. "Men and Women Never to Be Forgotten."
Christian Science Monitor (14 May), p. 11.
      Frederick Douglass is the vivid story of Douglass'
younger years--born in a slave cabin, teaching himself
to read, and finally escaping to the North.

16   VIGUERS, RUTH HILL. Review of Frederick Douglass. The Horn
Book Magazine, 35 (August), 293-94.
      Bontemps emphasizes Douglass' youth, covering his later
years only briefly in the two final chapters. The story
of Douglass' slavery, escape, and education is exciting
material and Bontemps tells his story with a restraint
that allows the facts to speak for themselves.

1960 A BOOKS - NONE

WRITINGS ABOUT ARNA WENDELL BONTEMPS, 1926-1976

1960 B SHORTER WRITINGS

*1   ANON. Review of Frederick Douglass: Slave, Fighter, Freeman.
     Negro Educational Review, 11 (July), 139.
          Listed in Hallie Q. Brown Memorial Library. Index to
     Periodical Articles by and about Negroes. Boston: G. K.
     Hall, vol. 11.

2   BLOS, JOAN WINSOR. "Importance of the Cherry Tree." The
     Saturday Review, 43 (20 February), 40.
          Bontemps presents social history as well as the personal
     life in this biography, Frederick Douglass. He subtly
     makes the point that slavery is wrong whether or not it
     is coupled with physical cruelty.

3   MAJOR, GERRI. "Society World." Jet (3 November), p. 3.
          A brief note on Bontemps' receipt of a Ford Foundation
     grant to study African culture in Kenya.

1961 A BOOKS - NONE

1961 B SHORTER WRITINGS

1   ANON. Review of 100 Years of Negro Freedom. Kirkus Reviews,
     29 (15 March), 296.
          By bringing out the personalities of the various Negro
     leaders with whom he deals, Bontemps gives a "warm and
     wholesome" tone to this history of the first hundred years
     since the abolition of slavery. Many little-known facts
     are revealed, and generally, "the cause of human equality
     is well served by this level-headed backward glance" over
     the past century.

2   ANON. "Recent Books: A Selection." The Bookmark, 20 (June),
     207.
          Bontemps, "an accomplished writer," has made a "valuable
     contribution" with this popular history of the years since
     the Emancipation, 100 Years of Negro Freedom.

*3   ANON. Review of 100 Years of Negro Freedom. San Francisco
     Chronicle (11 June), p. 27.
          Listed in Book Review Digest.

4   ANON. Review of 100 Years of Negro Freedom. The Booklist,
     57 (1 July), 653.
          Bontemps, a Fisk University librarian, presents an account
     of Negro intellectual, political, and cultural leaders

of the 100 years following emancipation. The book is
carefully researched and lively.

5   ANON. Review of 100 Years of Negro Freedom. The Crisis, 68
    (August-September), 456.
        Bontemps uses his novelistic skill to make this history
    of the Negro come alive. He tells the story of the race
    through the lives of its heroes and leaders--people like
    Frederick Douglass, Booker T. Washington, W. E. B. DuBois,
    and Walter White.

6   BRICKMAN, WILLIAM W. Review of 100 Years of Negro Freedom.
    School and Society, 89 (16 December), 441.
        This dramatic story of the Negro's history since Emanci-
    pation is told through the lives of leaders of the race.
    While some lesser-known figures are treated interestingly
    along with traditional leaders, other well-known figures
    are "treated in cursory fashion."

7   REDDING, SAUNDERS. "In the Vanguard of Civil Rights." The
    Saturday Review, 44 (12 August), 34.
        While Bontemps is an expert writer, he does not quite
    "pull the strands together" as he attempts to tell the
    story of 100 Years of Negro Freedom by telling the story
    of the leaders of the race. Part of the problem is the
    people he chooses as leaders and his attitude toward them.
    For example, when he writes of Booker T. Washington, Bon-
    temps is torn between the desire to present him as a hero
    and the desire to debunk him. Nevertheless, the book is
    significant and exciting.

8   SCHUYLER, GEORGE S. "Long Century, Long Road." New York
    Herald Tribune Books (3 September), p. 9.
        100 Years of Negro Freedom does a great deal to expose
    the unfairness under which the Negro has labored during
    and after the Civil War. Unfortunately, Bontemps says
    little or nothing about many important facets of the Negro
    movement: organized labor, black capitalism, due largely
    to Tuskegee's teachings, and the "Go to High School--Go
    to College" educational movement. He is also grossly un-
    fair to Booker T. Washington. "While the book is entertain-
    ing and absorbing," it could have been far more complete.

9   STRONG, AUGUSTA. "The Long Road." Freedomways, 1 (Fall),
    344-46.
        Bontemps' 100 Years of Negro Freedom is not a complete
    history, nor is it scholarly, but it is an impressive,

valuable, accurate book. Bontemps uses his skills as librarian and novelist to best advantage in this provoca- tive book, which is simple enough for the teenager yet challenging enough for adults.

1962 A BOOKS - NONE

1962 B SHORTER WRITINGS

*1   ANON. Review of 100 Years of Negro Freedom. Community, 21
     (February), 14.
          Listed in Hallie Q. Brown Memorial Library. Index to
     Periodical Articles by and about Negroes. Boston: G. K.
     Hall, vol. 13.

2   SWENSON, RUTH P. Review of 100 Years of Negro Freedom. Wis-
     consin Library Bulletin, 58 (May), 171.
          Bontemps "recounts the story [of black history since
     Emancipation] in terms of the leaders, their beliefs and
     their contributions. A useful book for reading and refer-
     ence, this belongs in all public library collections."

1963 A BOOKS - NONE

1963 B SHORTER WRITINGS

1   ANON. Review of American Negro Poetry. Negro Digest, 12
     (September), 52.
          A good, comprehensive anthology even though the "quality
     of the poetry is not uniformly excellent." Bontemps in-
     cludes a good blending of older established poets with new
     writers who have never been included in anthologies before.

2   ANON. Review of American Negro Poetry. The Crisis, 70
     (October), 509.
          Bontemps includes the work of 56 poets from Dunbar to
     modern writers. The poems "reflect the warmth and spon-
     taneity of American Negroes."

3   MORSE, CARL. "All Have Something to Say." New York Times
     Book Review (6 October), pp. 4, 28.
          There are two traditions in black poetry--the folk,
     represented by blues and spirituals, and formal poetry.
     American Negro Poetry is made up of the latter. As one
     reads the earlier poets included, such as Paul Laurence
     Dunbar, James Weldon Johnson, Angelina Grimké, it is sur-

1963

prising how much they sound like the polite American poets of the Victorian era. Later, the Harlem Renaissance poets seem to echo Millay, Sandburg, and e. e. cummings. Langston Hughes is really the only first-rate poet in this period, although Jean Toomer is interesting. Of the later poets, Robert Hayden, Gwendolyn Brooks, LeRoi Jones, and a few others write good poetry. On the whole, this is a disappointing collection.

4   PARIS, JAMES REID. Review of American Negro Poetry. Library Journal, 88 (July), 2708.
       While this is a good collection, it is not as complete as the earlier The Poetry of the Negro, co-edited by Bontemps. However, it is a good mixture of the standard black poets such as Langston Hughes and Countee Cullen with some eighteen new poets. The variety of the poetry and the editor's introduction make the collection interesting and valuable.

5   SCOGGIN, MARGARET C. Review of American Negro Poetry. The Horn Book Magazine, 39 (October), 521.
       This anthology ranges over the last seventy years, from Paul Laurence Dunbar to LeRoi Jones, and mingles representative poems of well-known poets such as Langston Hughes and Gwendolyn Brooks with younger poets of recent years. "Interesting, valuable, up-to-date."

6   STEPANCHEV, STEPHEN. "A Negro Anthology" in "Chorus of Versemakers: A Mid-1963 Medley." New York Herald Tribune Books (11 August), p. 6.
       Bontemps' American Negro Poetry, including 55 poets who published over the last seventy years, shows the growing competence and sophistication of black poets in this century. Most notable are the poets who have become prominent since 1945--poets such as Melvin Tolson, Owen Dodson, Margaret Walker, Gwendolyn Brooks, and LeRoi Jones. The other notable thing is how many black poets choose to treat universal themes unrelated to race.

1964 A BOOKS - NONE

1964 B SHORTER WRITINGS

1   BARR, DONALD. "A Great Issue Confronts the Writer--and Haunts Us All." New York Times Book Review Children's Book Section (1 November), pp. 3, 54-55.

1965

Instead of serving up mere pap, children's books should
deal with real issues of the day, as do books treated in
this review essay. Bontemps' Famous Negro Athletes is an
"image-making" book which derives considerable melodrama
from the careers of sports greats such as Joe Louis, Satchel
Paige, and Jesse Owens. Yet this is a necessary sort of
book for our time.

2   NERNEY, JERALINE N. Review of Famous Negro Athletes. Library
    Journal, 89 (15 October), 4202-4203.
        This group of short biographies outlines the lives of
    well-known black athletes in truthful, unsentimental fashion,
    emphasizing the personal and professional difficulties faced
    by men and women such as Joe Louis, Willie Mays, and Althea
    Gibson.

1965 A BOOKS - NONE

1965 B SHORTER WRITINGS

1   ANON. Review of Famous Negro Athletes. The Booklist, 61
    (15 March), 710-11.
        Bontemps, a prominent black author, presents short biog-
    raphies of nine black athletes, emphasizing their youth and
    the hardships each endured on the way to success in his or
    her chosen sport. Included are Joe Louis, Jackie Robinson,
    Jesse Owens, Althea Gibson.

2   ANON. Review of American Negro Poetry. Bibliographical Survey:
    The Negro in Print, 1, no. 1 (May), 11.
        Good selection covering approximately seventy years.

3   ANON. Review of Chariot in the Sky: A Story of the Jubilee
    Singers. Bibliographical Survey: The Negro in Print, 1,
    no. 3 (September), 15.
        Treats history of the Fisk singers through semi-fiction-
    alized story of Caleb Willows, one of the original singers.

4   ANON. Review of Famous Negro Athletes. Bulletin of the Center
    for Children's Books, 19, no. 1 (September), 3-4.
        Bontemps treats the personal lives of famous Negro ath-
    letes as well as their careers in sports. While it contains
    popular subject matter the book is weakened by an overly
    artificial style. Recommended for collections that are
    weak in Afro-American holdings.

1965

5   ANON. Review of The Story of the Negro. Bibliographical Sur-
     vey: The Negro in Print, 1, no. 3 (September), 16.
         A history of the black race in America from the intro-
     duction of slavery in 1619.

6   BONE, ROBERT A. "Aspects of the Racial Past," in his The
     Negro Novel in America. Revised edition. New Haven and
     London: Yale University Press, pp. 120-23.
         Treats Bontemps as "a transitional figure whose novels
     bear the mark both of the Negro Renaissance and of the
     depression years which follow." Before turning to fiction,
     Bontemps was "a minor poet." While God Sends Sunday is a
     definite product of the Renaissance, the two historical
     novels Black Thunder and Drums at Dusk reflect the rebel-
     lious attitude of the 1930's. Because of its strength in
     characterization and the deft use of symbolism, Black Thun-
     der is considerably superior to Bontemps' other two novels.
     See 1958.B1.

1966 A BOOKS - NONE

1966 B SHORTER WRITINGS

1   ANON. Review of Anyplace But Here. Bibliographical Survey:
     The Negro in Print, 1, no. 5 (January), 2.
         Studies the four periods of migration from the South:
     antebellum escapes, the era following Emancipation, and
     the two world wars. Stresses the contributions of the
     migrants.

2   ANON. Review of We Have Tomorrow. Bibliographical Survey:
     The Negro in Print, 1, no. 5 (January), 20.
         Biographical sketches of twelve Negroes who made signi-
     ficant progress by entering jobs and professions normally
     closed to the race.

3   ANON. Review of Anyplace But Here. Kirkus Reviews, 34
     (1 February), 171-72.
         While this book is not as well organized as it could
     have been, the material it contains is valuable enough to
     redeem it. Covering Negro migrations of the nineteenth
     and twentieth centuries, Bontemps and Jack Conroy "fill
     the gap in American Negro history which white America has
     permitted to exist."

4   ANON. Review of Famous Negro Athletes. Bibliographical Sur-
     vey: The Negro in Print, 1, no. 6 (March), 14.

1966

Traces the rise of Joe Louis, Sugar Ray Robinson, Jackie Robinson, "Satchel" Paige, Jesse Owens, Wilt Chamberlain and others.

*5 ANON. Review of Anyplace But Here. Kirkus Reviews, 34 (1 March), 256.
      Listed in Book Review Index.

6 ANON. Review of Anyplace But Here. Library Journal, 91 (15 June), 3270.
      Brief recommendation of book for young adults. This revised edition of They Seek A City (1945) is valuable not only for its information on the black migration to major cities but for biographical notes on important black figures from the lesser-known DuSable to famous figures such as Malcolm X. The revision has resulted in a much more comprehensive study of the Great Migration.

7 ANON. Review of Anyplace But Here. Bibliographical Survey: The Negro in Print, 2, no. 3 (September), 18.
      Updates the authors' previous work They Seek A City by including recent prominent black leaders such as Marcus Garvey and Malcolm X, and by including coverage of conflicts in Watts, Detroit, and other areas.

8 ANON. Review of Anyplace But Here. Choice, 3 (October), 722.
      Although the growth of this book over the years (it was originally published as They Seek A City in an earlier edition) and its joint authorship result in "unevenness of text and variation in viewpoint," the book is still valuable for the insight it offers into the background of recent race riots such as that in Watts. Recommended for college libraries even if they already have They Seek A City.

9 ANON. Review of Anyplace But Here. Sepia, 15 (October), 71.
      This book, a revised edition of the authors' 1945 book They Seek A City, "is filled with human-interest accounts of little-known and famous Negroes." It treats Negro migrations from the Civil War to the present, but manages to do so in interesting human terms.

10 ANON. Review of the record "An Anthology of Negro Poetry for Young People." Bibliographical Survey: The Negro in Print, 2, no. 4 (November), 24.
      Bontemps reads poetry of Paul Laurence Dunbar, Langston Hughes, Countee Cullen, Claude McKay, himself and others.

.11 EDITORS OF EBONY. "Arna Wendell Bontemps," in The Negro Handbook. Chicago: Johnson Publishing Company, p. 396.

1966

> Brief biography and partial list of works. Also contains brief descriptive notes on the following works: <u>Story of the Negro</u> (p. 185); <u>Famous Negro Athletes</u> and <u>100 Years of Negro Freedom</u> (p. 193); <u>American Negro Poetry</u> (p. 196); and <u>The Poetry of the Negro</u> (p. 197).

12 HUGHES, LANGSTON. "The Negro and American Entertainment," in <u>The American Negro Reference Book</u>. Edited by John P. Davis. Englewood Cliffs, New Jersey: Prentice-Hall, Inc., pp. 842, 848.

> Bontemps' collaboration with Countee Cullen on the adaptation of <u>St. Louis Woman</u> from <u>God Sends Sunday</u> is briefly commented on. Harold Arlen and Johnny Mercer took the resulting book and turned it into a successful musical comedy.

13 KATZ, WILLIAM. "Much Yet to Overcome." <u>The Saturday Review</u>, 49 (13 August), 26-27.

> <u>Anyplace But Here</u> is an exciting collection of stories telling of black people who made up the movement known as the Negro migration. Stemming from research that Bontemps and Jack Conroy began as writers for the Illinois W.P.A. writer's project, this book updates material published by the authors in their 1945 work <u>They Seek A City</u>. In many areas they cover, the authors have done more thorough research than anyone else in the field. Historically, the book runs from DuSable's founding of a fort on the site of present-day Chicago to the activities of the Black Muslims. An essential book for libraries and for the high school and college classroom.

14 LITTLEJOHN, DAVID. "Before Native Son: The Renaissance and After," in his <u>Black on White: A Critical Survey of Writing by American Negroes</u>. New York: Viking Press, pp. 50, 62-65.

> Bontemps is not really successful except as a poet. <u>God Sends Sunday</u> is a "sugary, harmless version of [the Renaissance] spirit," and the two historical novels of the thirties are "dismal"; his attempts at play scripts produced "nothing memorable." But some of his love poems and his "Southern Mansion" are good, especially the latter--"a small must for everyone's collection."

15 McANDREW, BRUNO, O.S.B. Review of <u>Anyplace But Here</u>. <u>Best Sellers</u>, 26, no. 7 (1 July), 135.

> In spite of the noble intentions of its authors, <u>Anyplace But Here</u> is not a complete success. The older material of <u>They Seek A City</u> (1945) is not successfully integrated with

the recent additions and the result is a lack of clear
focus in the present work. The material on recent ghetto
riots is most interesting and might have produced a far
better book if treated alone.

16   MARGOLIES, EDWARD. Review of Anyplace But Here. Library
        Journal, 91 (1 April), 1888-89.
           Like Bontemps and Conroy's 1945 book They Seek A City,
        this work traces the migration of Negroes from the South
        to the inhospitable North. In spite of the fact that it
        sometimes over-emphasizes obvious shortcomings of the north-
        ern cities and their populations, the book does give insight
        into the origins and growth of black nationalist movements
        from Garveyism to the riots in Watts. More careful docu-
        mentation would have made the book even more helpful al-
        though the authors' sources are listed in a comprehensive
        bibliography.

1967 A BOOKS - NONE

1967 B SHORTER WRITINGS

1   ANON. Review of The Story of George Washington Carver.
        Bibliographical Survey: The Negro in Print, 2, no. 5
        (January), 13.
           Follows Carver from slavery through his struggles to
        obtain an education and on to national prominence as a
        scientist. For young readers.

*2   ANON. Review of Anyplace But Here. American Book Collector,
        17 (Summer), 3.
           Listed in Book Review Index.

3   ANON. Review of Lonesome Boy. Kirkus Reviews, 35 (15 Septem-
        ber), 1137.
           This "haunting story" might have been ahead of its time
        when it was first published in 1954 but "should find an
        audience now."

4   ANON. Review of Lonesome Boy. Publishers' Weekly, 192,
        no. 18 (30 October), 50.
           Houghton Mifflin is to be praised for reissuing this
        memorable book, which is as moving now as when it was first
        published.

5   DICKINSON, DONALD C. A Bio-bibliography of Langston Hughes:
        1902-1967. Hamden, Connecticut: Archon Books, pp. 62-63,
        106.

1967

        Describes Hughes' and Bontemps' collaboration on their juvenile book <u>Popo and Fifina</u> and their anthology <u>The Poetry of the Negro, 1746-1949</u>.

6   GAVER, MARY V. "Realism and Children's Books." <u>Teachers College Record</u>, 68 (February), 452.
        Stresses Bontemps' insistence on reality--particularly the plight of the lonely child--in his own books, <u>Sad-Faced Boy</u> and <u>Lonesome Boy</u>. Adults misjudge children when they assume that they are not ready or not interested in literature that faces reality.

7   HEILBRUN, CAROLYN. "Repeat Performances." <u>New York Times Book Review: Part II, Children's Books</u> (5 November), p. 59.
        <u>Lonesome Boy</u> is a welcome revival--a haunting story about a young trumpet player.

8   MITCHELL, LOFTEN. "Fear and War: The Nineteen-Forties," in his <u>Black Drama</u>. New York: Hawthorn Books, pp. 128-29.
        Brief account of the collaboration of Bontemps with Countee Cullen in the writing of <u>St. Louis Woman</u>, a dramatization of <u>God Sends Sunday</u>.

9   NELSON, B. H. Review of <u>Anyplace But Here</u>. <u>Journal of Negro History</u>, 52 (January), 76-78.
        Directed at a general audience, this revision of the authors' 1945 work <u>They Seek A City</u> deals with the people who have made up the Negro migration. "Good history can, at the same time, be good literature. Bontemps and Conroy have written both."

10   RANDALL, DUDLEY. Review of <u>Anyplace But Here</u>. <u>Negro Digest</u>, 16 (August), 51.
        This book is a new version of <u>They Seek A City</u> (1945), effectively brought up to date with chapters on the Watts, Chicago, and Harlem riots. Two small errors in the section on Detroit are pointed out.

1968 A BOOKS - NONE

1968 B SHORTER WRITINGS

1   ANON. Review of <u>Lonesome Boy</u>. <u>Best Sellers</u>, 27, no. 19 (1 January), 391.
        Although it is a handsomely illustrated volume, this reissue of Arna Bontemps' 1955 work is not really as good as earlier reviewers thought and seems over-priced.

1969

1969 A BOOKS - NONE

1969 B SHORTER WRITINGS

1   ANON. Review of Black Thunder. Bibliographical Survey: The
    Negro in Print, 4, no. 5 (January), 1.
        Bontemps popularizes the history of Gabriel Prosser, a
    slave rebel of the early 19th century.

2   M., N. "Poetry for teens--and older." Christian Science
    Monitor (6 November), p. B 10.
        Hold Fast to Dreams, a collection of memorable poems,
    is "a bargain at $3.95." The absence of notes on the poets
    is good in its way; there is nothing to distract us from
    the poetry itself.

3   NEVINS, ALLAN. Review of Great Slave Narratives. The Saturday
    Review, 52 (6 December), 60.
        The narratives in this volume are carefully selected and
    Bontemps provides a scholarly and thoughtful introduction
    to them. The narratives of Gustavus Vassa and James Penning-
    ton are particularly vigorous and exciting.

4   OBOLER, ELI M. Review of Hold Fast to Dreams: Poems Old and
    New. Library Journal, 94 (August), 2796.
        Bontemps has compiled an uneven collection ranging from
    overly sentimental poetry to masterpieces, but the major
    part of the contents is of high quality. Not only well-
    known poets but lesser ones are represented and the collec-
    tion is notable for its blending of black and white poets
    from all ages. On balance, the anthology is highly readable.

5   ROBINSON, WILHELMINA S. "Bontemps, Arna: Author," in her
    Historical Negro Biographies. New York: Publishers Com-
    pany, Inc., pp. 164-65.
        Thumbnail biography of Bontemps and a listing of a few
    of his works.

6   RODMAN, SELDEN. "Poetry: A Collection of Collections." New
    York Times Book Review: Part II, Children's Books (9 Novem-
    ber), p. 7.
        Bontemps' Hold Fast to Dreams is a disappointing antholo-
    gy made up of the work of "black verse-smiths," "old chest-
    nuts of social revolt" and poems that have been "antholo-
    gized to death."

7   SCHUMAN, PATRICIA. Review of Great Slave Narratives. Library
    Journal, 94 (15 September), 3056.

1969

The narratives in this volume do an excellent job of
bringing history to life through the personal reminiscences
of slaves who experienced it. Not only are the stories of
Olandah Equianor (Gustavus Vassa), James Pennington, and
William and Ellen Craft interesting as history, but they
show a surprising literary quality as well.

8   SEACORD, LAURA F.   Review of Hold Fast to Dreams. Library
    Journal, 94 (15 September), 117-19.
        Bontemps has produced a very personal anthology which
    ranges from commonly anthologized poets such as Wordsworth,
    through the standard poets of the 1920's, and into the work
    of less well-known writers of the twentieth century, most
    notably younger black poets.

9   VIGUERS, RUTH HILL.   Review of Hold Fast to Dreams. The Horn
    Book Magazine, 45 (August), 419.
        Bontemps, a poet himself, has selected a wide range of
    poems by authors of various cultures and races. These are
    poems Bontemps found he "couldn't forget," and young read-
    ers will find some they will always remember also.

10 WEISBERGER, BERNARD A.   Review of Great Slave Narratives.
    Chicago Tribune Book World, 3, no. 36 (7 September), 5.
        Great Slave Narratives, like Puttin' on Ole Massa edited
    by Gilbert Osofsky, offers the modern reader a significant
    picture of slavery as it was viewed by the slave. While it
    is hard to consider such books objectively at present, they
    record a history that will be increasingly valuable when
    readers can look back on the past more dispassionately.

1970 A BOOKS - NONE

1970 B SHORTER WRITINGS

1   ANON.   Review of Great Slave Narratives. The Booklist, 66
    (15 January), 576, 578.
        In introducing these three narratives, Bontemps empha-
    sizes their importance in the nineteenth century and their
    effects on later prose writing by black authors. The nar-
    ratives which follow are "of human interest as well as
    historical importance."

2   ANON.   Review of Hold Fast to Dreams. American Libraries, 1
    (April), 384.
        "Inviting anthology representing the personal preferences
    of a Negro writer."

1971

3   BELL, MABEL BOYD. "Recent Children's Books." <u>Top of the News</u>,
    26 (January), 207.
        Bontemps, "a distinguished black author," presents his
    favorite poems in <u>Hold Fast to Dreams</u>, "a wonderful book
    for browsing."

4   COOK, MERCER. Review of <u>Great Slave Narratives</u>. <u>The Journal</u>
    <u>of Negro History</u>, 55 (January), 82-83.
        An excellent selection of three of the best slave nar-
    ratives, with a good introduction by its distinguished
    editor.

5   CURSHMAN, JEROME. Review of <u>The Poetry of the Negro:</u>
    <u>1746-1970</u>. Revised edition. <u>Library Journal</u>, 95 (1 Novem-
    ber), 3786.
        Although Langston Hughes and Arna Bontemps have not re-
    vised the introduction of their 1949 anthology, they have
    brought the present edition up to date by adding the works
    of some 65 contemporary poets. These additions have resulted
    in a good survey of black poetry to modern times.

6   KIMBALL, JEFFREY. Review of <u>Great Slave Narratives</u>. <u>Negro</u>
    <u>History Bulletin</u>, 33 (November), 178.
        While Bontemps' selections are good--he picks Gustavus
    Vassa, James Pennington, and William and Ellen Craft--he
    fails to analyze the narratives from a sociological or his-
    torical point of view, and his comments on their literary
    importance are inadequate. The texts themselves are not
    footnoted, nor is there an index or bibliography. This is
    a valuable contribution but could have been better edited.

7   [SMELTZER], SISTER M. ETHELDREDA. Review of <u>The Story of George</u>
    <u>Washington Carver</u>. <u>Catholic Library World</u>, 41 (January),
    320.
        Summarizes the story of Carver's early life. "An appeal-
    ing story of his kind acts and scientific discoveries."

8   _____. Review of <u>Hold Fast to Dreams</u>. <u>Catholic Library World</u>,
    41 (April), 535.
        This anthology of the favorite poems of Arna Bontemps--
    himself a poet as well as a teacher--will "greatly enrich
    a collection--even a large one in any library."

<u>1971 A BOOKS - NONE</u>

1971

1971 B SHORTER WRITINGS

1   ANON. Review of Free At Last: The Life of Frederick Douglass.
     Kirkus Reviews, 39 (15 February), 204-205.
          Bontemps chooses to emphasize Douglass' role as an
     abolitionist at the expense of his years as a slave and,
     more significantly, his life after the Civil War. "Worst
     of all is the generally short shrift given to Frederick
     Douglass' intellectual achievements." While the book is
     aimed at young adult readers, "Douglass deserves far better
     than he has gotten here."

2   ANON. Review of Great Slave Narratives. Bibliographical Sur-
     vey: The Negro in Print, 6, no. 5 (March), 1.
          Bontemps notes the importance of the slave narrative
     as a genre, stressing its contribution to cultural history
     and its influence on later authors.

3   ANON. Review of Mr. Kelso's Lion. Bulletin of the Center
     for Children's Books, 24, no. 7 (March), 102-103.
          While the plot has good possibilities, Bontemps fails
     to develop it as completely as he might. The story needs
     more focus; the style, intended for grades 3 and 4, is ade-
     quate. Book is given only a "marginal" rating.

4   ANON. Review of Free at Last. Choice, 8 (September), 901.
          In this popularization of the early life of Frederick
     Douglass, Bontemps employs fictional techniques such as
     the flashback, which he handles a bit awkwardly at times.
     He also sensationalizes by stressing the dramatic events
     of Douglass' life. While he has used Douglass' autobiogra-
     phies as sources, it is difficult to find the exact sources
     of some incidents. Useful for general readers but not for
     scholars.

5   ANON. Review of Chariot in the Sky. Kirkus Reviews, 39
     (15 October), 1133.
          This revised edition of Bontemps' 1951 book about the
     Fisk University Jubilee Singers seems curiously non-militant
     today, but Caleb Willows, its protagonist, is still "engag-
     ingly admirable," and the book is still informative and
     relevant.

6   BARDOLPH, RICHARD. The Negro Vanguard. First published in
     1959. Westport, Connecticut: Negro Universities Press,
     pp. 151, 153, 156, 214, 276, 356, 362.
          A collection of significant biographical notes on Bon-
     temps, noting what experiences and backgrounds he had in
     common with various successful contemporaries.

1971

7   BENNETT, STEPHEN B. and WILLIAM W. NICHOLS. "Violence in
    Afro-American Fiction: An Hypothesis." Modern Fiction
    Studies, 17 (Summer), 221-28.
        Discussion of the suicide in "A Summer Tragedy" as part
    of a larger pattern in the works of Afro-American fiction
    writers such as James Baldwin, Ralph Ellison, Richard Wright,
    and Chester Himes. Only in violence and death do black men
    discover their humanity. Thus, the Pattons' suicide is
    their only meaningful act in a long life of merely existing.

8   FULLER, HOYT. "Books by Arna Bontemps." Black World, 20,
    no. 11 (September), 78-79.
        Brief dedication statement. Bibliography of Bontemps'
    works up to 1971. This issue of Black World is dedicated
    to Bontemps and features a cover photo.

9   HOWARD, VICTOR B. Review of Five Black Lives: The Autobiogra-
    phies of Venture Smith, James Mars, William Grimes, G. W.
    Offley, and James L. Smith. New England Quarterly, 44
    (December), 685-87.
        These narratives are well chosen and perceptively intro-
    duced. It is noteworthy that Bontemps chose writers who
    did not rely on white collaborators in writing their stories;
    while some awkwardness results when unlettered people tell
    their own stories, the book has an authenticity and energy
    often missing from slave narratives.

10 KUGLER, RUBEN. Review of Free at Last: The Life of Frederick
    Douglass. Library Journal, 96 (15 April), 1358.
        While it is less scholarly than Benjamin Quarles' Fred-
    erick Douglass, Free at Last is more readable, and is a
    helpful supplement to Douglass' own autobiographies.

11 McPHERSON, JAMES M., LAURENCE B. HOLLAND, JAMES M. BANNER,
    NANCY J. WEISS, and MICHAEL D. BELL. Blacks in America:
    Bibliographical Essays. Garden City, New York: Doubleday
    and Company, 430 pp., passim.
        Lists many of Bontemps' works under historical, biogra-
    phical, and literary topics.

12 MURRAY, MARGUERITE M. Review of Mr. Kelso's Lion. Library
    Journal, 96 (15 March), 1114.
        The rather inconclusive plot of this juvenile book, in-
    tended for third and fourth grade children, is redeemed by
    the warmth of the relationship between Percy and his grand-
    father, about whom the story revolves.

13 ODELL, BRIAN NEAL. Review of Free at Last. America, 125
    (16 October), 295-96.

1971

> "We read much--real or imagined--in Free at Last of Fred-
> erick Douglass the man of anger, passion and resentment; but
> we see little of Frederick Douglass the thinker, the writer,
> the political strategist." Bontemps emphasizes Douglass'
> "more 'salable' characteristics," and his book therefore
> appears "incomplete, and at worst deceitful."

14 PLOSKI, HARRY A., OTTO J. LINDENMEYER, ERNEST KAISER, eds.
   "Arna Bontemps: Poet, novelist, dramatist," in Reference
   Library of Black America. Volume III. New York: Bell-
   wether Publishing Company, p. 4.
   Brief sketch of Bontemps' life and works, the latter
   under the headings of poetry, fiction, history and children's
   literature.

15 WEIL, DOROTHY. "Folklore Motifs in Arna Bontemps' Black
   Thunder." Southern Folklore Quarterly, 35 (March), 1-14.
   Bontemps uses folklore motifs very skillfully throughout
   Black Thunder to sustain interest, to help characterize the
   Black characters, and to add to the mood and the atmosphere
   he is trying to create. Burial customs, the reading of
   "signs" in nature, and the use of conjure are important
   folk elements in the novel.

1972 A BOOKS - NONE

1972 B SHORTER WRITINGS

1 ANON. Review of The Poetry of the Negro. Choice, 8 (January),
   1452-53.
   A very comprehensive anthology of poetry on black life,
   especially in the area of the Harlem Renaissance. The
   section of tributary poems by whites, while it might be
   successful as a separate anthology, does not belong in this
   volume, and the space saved could have been better used for
   more black poets or more poems by those who have only one
   representative poem. Some poets don't appear--Nikki Giovan-
   ni, Etheridge Knight, for example. But still, overall, the
   book is indispensable for any library.

2 ANON. Review of Chariot in the Sky. The Booklist, 68
   (15 January), 435.
   Bontemps' 1951 book on the Fisk Jubilee Singers has
   been reissued--the type has been re-set, chapter illustrations and map have been omitted, and the title-page illustration has been replaced with one "more in keeping with
   the times."

1972

3   ANON. Notice of The Harlem Renaissance Remembered. Library
       Journal, 97 (1 April), 1354.
           Bontemps begins with his own "The Awakening: A Memoir"
       and includes others' studies of W. E. B. DuBois, Jean Toom-
       er, Langston Hughes, Countee Cullen, Zora Neale Hurston.

4   ANON. Review of The Harlem Renaissance Remembered. Kirkus
       Reviews, 40 (1 June), 647.
           Much of the literary criticism in this anthology is
       "mediocre." In general, "an uneven collection."

5   ANON. Review of Young Booker. Kirkus Reviews, 40 (1 July),
       756.
           Most biographies of Washington have either glorified
       him or condemned him. Bontemps' recent biography "clearly
       belongs in the former category," as the author treats the
       early life of Washington and his struggles to establish
       Tuskegee. "As for Booker T. Washington, the private person-
       ality, this offers the blandest of chronological detail."
       Readers must still wait for a really definitive biography.

6   ANON. Review of The Harlem Renaissance Remembered. The Book-
       list, 69 (1 December), 323.
           This collection, introduced by a personal retrospective
       essay by Bontemps, the editor, offers critical views of
       the patterns of writing during the period and assessments
       of selected authors who emerged during the renaissance. It
       should prove valuable to students of Afro-American culture,
       history, and literature.

7   BONTEMPS, ARNA, ed. The Harlem Renaissance Remembered: Essays
       Edited with a Memoir. New York: Dodd, Mead and Company,
       310 pp., passim.
           Bontemps' role in the Harlem Renaissance is noted through-
       out the book but is discussed at length only in his own in-
       troduction, "The Awakening: A Memoir," pp. 1-26.

8   BRAXTON, JODI. "Asserting Selfhood." The New Republic, 167
       (4 November), 27-30.
           Discusses the individual essays in Harlem Renaissance
       Remembered, complaining that they lack a common thread
       that would tie all of the essays together. The book "is
       uneven, but the originality and excellence of a few of the
       essays, together with its fine bibliography, make it a
       real achievement."

9   CAVISTON, JOHN F. Review of Chariot in the Sky. Library
       Journal, 97 (15 April), 1612-13.

1972

This book, which first appeared twenty years ago, seems
dated. Slavery is "white-washed": the slave-owners seem
too kindly depicted and the slaves are accommodationists.
Caleb Willows, the main character, is "one-dimensional."
Furthermore, the black characters are referred to as "colored," not "black," a defect which makes the book "unaccept-
able" today.

10 CONDIT, D. P. Review of The Harlem Renaissance Remembered.
National Review, 24 (15 September), 1019.
Bontemps, a minor poet during the Renaissance, has made
a generally good if uneven selection of essays, but his own
"memoir" gives "only a hazy impression" of the people and
principles involved.

11 GILZINGER, DONALD, Jr. Review of The Harlem Renaissance Remembered. Library Journal, 97 (July), 2399.
This anthology is a useful supplement to Nathan Huggins'
recently published Harlem Renaissance; while Huggins' book
treats the social and philosophical background of the movement, Bontemps and his contributors deal exclusively with
literary figures of the Renaissance. Bontemps' own memoir
of the period is of special interest.

12 GRAY, MRS. JOHN G. Review of Chariot in the Sky. Best Sellers,
31, no. 22 (15 February), 521.
Bontemps seems to have understated his message deliber-
ately--a grave error in the opinion of this reviewer. While
the suffering and deprivation of the nine Jubilee Singers
may speak for itself for an adult audience, the young readers for whom the book is intended need more authorial guid-
ance than Bontemps provides.

13 [JOHNSTON, ALBERT H.] Review of Harlem Renaissance [sic].
Publishers' Weekly, 202, no. 1 (3 July), 32.
As a prominent participant in the Harlem Renaissance,
Bontemps is uniquely suited to be editor of a study of the
authors who are identified with the movement. His own introductory essay offers valuable reminiscences of the
period, while the twelve critical pieces that follow offer
a wealth of information.

14 _____. Review of Young Booker. Publishers' Weekly, 202,
no. 12 (18 September), 67.
Bontemps' portrayal of Booker T. Washington suffers
from a too-heavy reliance on Washington's Up From Slavery
and from oversimplification and superficiality. While it
reads easily, it is clearly intended as an inspiration for
young black readers, not as a serious study of the man and
his policies.

15 MALKIN, MARY ANN O'BRIAN. Review of Harlem Renaissance Remembered. A. B. Bookman's Yearbook edited by Sol. M. Malkin.
Newark, New Jersey: Specialist Book World, p. 11.
Brief description of book and excerpts of typical pas-
sages from Bontemps' own introduction.

16 MITCHELL, LOUIS D. Review of Harlem Renaissance Remembered.
Best Sellers, 32, no. 11 (1 September), 251.
This comprehensive collection of critical essays on the
major literary figures of the Harlem Renaissance would be
a valuable addition to any library. It documents the
achievements of authors such as Claude McKay, Jean Toomer,
Countee Cullen, Langston Hughes, Nella Larsen, and Zora
Neale Hurston in a way that makes them understandable to
this generation and those to come.

17 SIMMS, AURORA G. Review of Young Booker. Library Journal,
97 (15 October), 3306.
Young Booker seems to lack insight into the reasons for
Booker T. Washington's acquiescence to segregation and his
acceptance of white standards. To get a true picture of
Washington, the reader would have to read his own autobiographical Up From Slavery along with Bontemps' biography.

18 THOMPSON, G. R. "Themes, Topics, and Criticism," in American
Literary Scholarship: An Annual/ 1970. Edited by J. Al-
bert Robbins. Durham, North Carolina: Duke University
Press, pp. 395-96.
In his introductory essay to Great Slave Narratives,
Bontemps points out the importance of the slave narrative
as a means for black people to express their suffering and
as one of their unique contributions to American culture.
The slave narrative is the most effective early model of
prose writing for later black authors.

19 W., A. C. Review of Hold Fast to Dreams. Childhood Education,
48 (January), 208.
Hold Fast is "an outstanding collection of poetry, with
special emphasis on the moods and feelings of today's
youngsters."

1973 A BOOKS - NONE

1973 B SHORTER WRITINGS

*1 ANON. Review of Free at Last. Catholic Library World, 44
(February), 445.
Listed in Book Review Index.

Writings about Arna Wendell Bontemps, 1926-1976

2   ANON. Review of Young Booker. The Booklist, 69 (15 March), 711.
     Bontemps deals mainly with the period from Washington's
     boyhood as a slave to his delivery of the Atlanta Exposition
     Address in 1893 in this biography for children in grades 6
     to 9. While he is generally truthful, he emphasizes the
     positive facets of Washington's career and says little
     about details such as his three marriages.

3   ANON. Review of The Harlem Renaissance Remembered. Choice,
     10 (April), 286.
     This book, along with Huggins' Harlem Renaissance, is an
     excellent critical look at a period that has been too long
     overlooked. Well-documented with a good bibliography, the
     book "belongs in every school and college library."

4   ANON. Review of The Old South. Kirkus Reviews, 41 (1 June),
     616.
     In this collection of stories about the South, Bontemps
     falls "somewhere betwixt Uncle Remus and Richard Wright,
     perhaps on the closer side of Brer Rabbit than Black Boy."

5   ANON. "Arna Bontemps, Writer, 70, Dies." New York Times
     (6 June), p. 50.
     Reports Bontemps' death of a heart attack at his Nash-
     ville home, Monday, June 4, 1973. Lengthy account of his
     career as a writer, emphasizing his part in the Harlem
     Renaissance and his versatility as a writer of novels,
     anthologies, children's books, and histories.

6   ANON. Review of The Old South. Publishers' Weekly, 203,
     no. 25 (18 June), 66.
     The fourteen simple and moving stories in this posthum-
     ous volume present black life in the South without bitter-
     ness. Bontemps shows skill at characterization as well as
     keen insight into southern society.

7   ANON. "Obituary Note." Publishers' Weekly, 204, no. 2
     (9 July), 37.
     Obituary and very short review of Bontemps' career.

8   ANON. "Arna Bontemps, Versatile Writer." The Crisis, 80
     (August-September), 222.
     Praises Bontemps as a writer of distinction who produced
     poems, novels, plays, and histories. He was "one of the
     most prolific and versatile writers of a memorable period
     in the development of Afro-American culture...."

9   ANON. "Young Readers Lose a Friend and Mentor: Arna Bontemps,
     1902-1973." Wilson Library Bulletin, 48 (October), 138.

Writings about Arna Wendell Bontemps, 1926-1976

1973

Account of memorial service for Bontemps in New York City,
20 June 1973. Emphasizes Bontemps' service as a librarian
and his writing for children.

10   BAKER, HOUSTON A., Jr. "Arna Bontemps: A Memoir." Black
      World, 22, no. 11 (September), 4-9.
            Portrait of Bontemps as teacher, scholar, man of letters,
      and friend. Emphasizes the neglect from which Bontemps'
      work suffered from the 1930's to the early 1960's.

11   BRACEY, JOHN H., Jr. Review of Young Booker. New York Times
      Book Review (4 March), pp. 34-35.
            Bontemps hews fairly close to Washington's own story of
      his life as related in Up From Slavery in this "readable
      popular account." Although Bontemps avoids the questions
      that might arise about some of Washington's actions, the
      book is a success on its own terms.

12   BROWN, STERLING A. "Arna Bontemps: Co-Worker, Comrade."
      Black World, 22, no. 11 (September), 11, 91-97.
            Bontemps deserves to be known much better than he has
      been, especially for his masterpiece, the novel Black Thunder.
      Critics black and white have too long neglected this impor-
      tant work and by doing so have lost sight of a major author.
      God Sends Sunday (1931) is also a worthwhile novel which
      has been badly understood, especially by David Littlejohn
      and Robert A. Bone. As a popular writer, Bontemps was
      often derivative almost to the point of plagiarism, yet
      the very volume of his work is astounding. His poetry
      is technically admirable, but its real strength is in its
      "meditative" quality. No one will replace Arna Bontemps.

13   CHAMBERLAIN, GARY L. "On Being Black and Being American."
      America, 128 (20 January), 42-43.
            Bontemps' collection of essays on the Harlem Renaissance
      is "an evocative and provocative picture of that great
      period of black arts." Not only does Bontemps capture the
      artistic excitement of the times in his introductory essay,
      but Harlem Renaissance Remembered as a whole stresses the
      important influences that have lingered.

14   JONES, VIRGINIA LACY. "Arna Bontemps: 1902-1973." Library
      Journal, 98 (July), 2038.
            Obituary and succinct biographical sketch of Bontemps,
      mentioning most of his literary works.

15   _____. "Arna Bontemps (1902-1973)." Library Journal, 98
      (September), 2599-2600.
            Condensation of above obituary, 1973.B14.

1973

16 MITCHELL, LOUIS D. Review of The Old South. Best Sellers,
    33, no. 17 (1 December), 385-86.
        This final published work by Bontemps exemplifies his
    strengths as a writer of fiction. The author's polished
    style creates, in these fourteen stories, an unforgettable
    picture of Negro and white life in the South of the 1930's.

17 O'BRIEN, JOHN. "Arna Bontemps," in his Interviews With Black
    Writers. New York: Liveright, pp. [2]-15.
        O'Brien questions Bontemps on a wide variety of matters,
    eliciting important reactions on the Harlem Renaissance
    and the authors whose works made up the renaissance, on
    the black aesthetic, on white resistance to black writers,
    on black expatriate writers, on the contemporary literary
    scene, and on his own works, particularly Black Thunder
    and the poems of Personals.

18 PERKINS, HUEL D. Review of The Harlem Renaissance Remembered.
    Black World, 22, no. 5 (March), 72-73.
        This is the best book yet on the Harlem Renaissance,
    partly because it addresses itself to the evaluation of the
    literary renaissance, not to social and historical questions,
    and partly because its editor, Bontemps, was a participant.
    Biographical notes on the contributors would have been one
    helpful addition.

19 PHILLIPS, FRANK LAMONT. "Necessitarianism: Elegy for Arna
    Wendell Bontemps." Black World, 22, no. 11 (September), 10.
    Twenty-nine line free verse poem on Bontemps' death.

20 SCHRAUFNAGEL, NOEL. "Before Native Son," in his From Apology
    to Protest: The Black American Novel. Deland, Florida:
    Everett Edwards, Inc., pp. 15-16.
        Although his first novel, God Sends Sunday, was "in the
    Van Vechten vogue," Bontemps shows greater independence of
    thought in his historical novels, Black Thunder and Drums
    at Dusk. Black Thunder, particularly, succeeds as "a
    comprehensive fictional portrayal of the slave insurrection
    of Gabriel Prosser."

21 SIMMS, AURORA G. Review of The Old South. Library Journal,
    98 (1 September), 2462.
        Bontemps' last work is a book of high literary quality
    and great social importance. Although modern readers may
    find these stories mild compared with the work of later
    protest writers, Bontemps was clearly one of the shapers
    of the modern black nationalist movement. The stories of
    The Old South are a rare combination of humor and deeper
    feelings.

22   THORNTON, HORTENSE E. Review of Harlem Renaissance Remembered.
      The Journal of Negro History, 58 (April), 214-17.
              Bontemps' collection of essays on the Harlem Renaissance
      is "the most comprehensive study of the literary facet...
      currently available in one text." Bontemps might have
      added a general introduction or at least a preface on the
      aims of the book, and brief statements about the contribu-
      tors would have been welcome. But overall, the book is
      indispensable.

23   YARDLEY, JONATHAN. Review of The Old South. New York Times
      Book Review (23 December), p. 11.
              Bontemps' fourteen stories seem "low-key, informal and
      chatty" at first, but there is more to them than one might
      notice on the first reading. While Bontemps writes honestly
      about the problems of race relations, he avoids bitterness.
      "Overall the stories convey a genuine love for the South."

24   YOUNG, JAMES O. Black Writers of the Thirties. Baton Rouge:
      Louisiana State University Press, pp. 135, 136, 154, 159,
      223-25.
              Brief discussions of Bontemps' use of folk materials and
      history in his three novels.

1974 A BOOKS - NONE

1974 B SHORTER WRITINGS

1   ANON. "Milestones in the Life of Arna Bontemps." American
      Libraries, 5 (December), 605.
              Chronological list of important dates in Bontemps' life,
      including educational history, publication of major works,
      literary awards, and teaching career.

2   BOGART, GARY. Review of The Old South. Wilson Library Bulletin,
      48 (March), 538.
              The fourteen stories in this collection offer the reader
      a large, varied set of characters. Their life-likeness and
      Bontemps' autobiographical introduction give the impression
      that he is writing of people he has known well. A rich book.

3   CONROY, JACK. "Memories of Arna Bontemps: Friend and Collab-
      orator." American Libraries, 5 (December), 602-606.
              Personal reminiscences of the long association between
      the author and Arna Bontemps, dating from 1938. Treats the
      origins of They Seek A City in considerable detail and
      describes their collaboration on children's books. Also

1974

includes brief critical commentary on the short story "A
Summer Tragedy" as a typical piece of Bontemps' fiction.
Reprinted 1976.B1.

4   COTTER, JAMES F. Review of American Negro Poetry, Revised
     edition. America, 131 (13 July), 19.
          This revision of Bontemps' 1963 anthology reflects great
     credit on its compiler; he is the best possible guide to
     the field. Among the twelve new poets added are some
     obviously significant writers: LeRoi Jones, Don L. Lee,
     and Nikki Giovanni.

5   DAVIS, ARTHUR P. "Arna Bontemps," in his From the Dark Tower:
     Afro-American Writers, 1900-1960. Washington, D.C.: Howard
     University Press, pp. 83-89.
          A short biographical essay on Bontemps is followed by
     separate discussions of his poetry, his fiction, and his
     writing for children. As a poet, Bontemps is less propa-
     gandistic and more obscure than most of his contemporaries
     and is always serious, meditative, never light. As a novel-
     ist, he did his best work in his second novel, Black Thunder,
     which conveys to the reader the spirit of resistance of
     Gabriel as black rebel. Bontemps is a true pioneer in
     writing for black children. Finally, while Davis does not
     discuss Bontemps' many anthologies, he stresses that they
     have "contributed greatly in the building of the under-
     standing and appreciation we now have of Negro literature."

6   DYBEK, CAREN. Review of Young Booker. English Journal, 63
     (January), 66.
          Bontemps tells Washington's life story vividly but with-
     out treating the complexities of his character that have
     been brought out by modern scholarship.

7   FRANKLIN, JOHN HOPE. "The Harlem Renaissance," in his From
     Slavery to Freedom: A History of Negro Americans. Fourth
     edition. New York: Alfred A. Knopf, pp. 383, 386.
          Briefly discusses Bontemps' poetry and his three novels
     as late contributions to the Harlem Renaissance.

8   TYMS, JAMES D. "The New Men." The New Republic, 170 (5 and
     12 January), 27-28.
          Bontemps "demonstrates great skill in capturing" the
     mood of the South in the 1930's in The Old South. Simply
     but sensitively he brings out the black experience of that
     time and place.

9 WHITLOW, ROGER. "1920-1940: The Harlem Renaissance and Its
   Influence," in his Black American Literature. Totowa, New
   Jersey: Littlefield, Adams and Company, pp. 100-103.
   Biographical sketch followed by a short discussion of
   Black Thunder, as Bontemps' "finest novel."

1975 A BOOKS - NONE

1975 B SHORTER WRITINGS

1 BONE, ROBERT. "Epilogue: Arna Bontemps," in his Down Home:
   A History of Afro-American Short Fiction from Its Beginnings
   to the End of the Harlem Renaissance. New York: G. P.
   Putnam's Sons, pp. 272-87.
   Outlines Bontemps' career and discusses the sketches and
   stories in The Old South. These stories are influenced by
   the pastoral mode and by folklore, preceding Bontemps'
   "turn to the left" of the later thirties, in which historical black rebellions furnish a dominant theme.

2 RUSH, THERESSA GUNNELS, CAROL FAIRBANKS MYERS, and ESTHER
   SPRING ARATA, eds. "Bontemps, Arna," in Black American
   Writers Past and Present: A Biographical and Bibliographical Dictionary. Vol. I. Metuchen, New Jersey: The
   Scarecrow Press, pp. 79-84.
   Brief biographical sketch of Bontemps, followed by a
   complete bibliography of his book-length works and some of
   his publications in periodicals, as well as a listing of
   some anthologies in which his work appears. A bibliography
   of secondary materials on Bontemps contains some errors,
   but is generally useful.

1976 A BOOKS - NONE

1976 B SHORTER WRITINGS

1 CONROY, JACK. "Memories of Arna Bontemps: Friend and Collabo-
   rator." Negro American Literature Forum, 10 (Summer), 53-57.
   Reprint of 1974.B3.

2 REDMOND, EUGENE B. "Minor, or Second-Echelon, Poets of the
   Renaissance," in his Drumvoices: The Mission of Afro-American Poetry. Garden City, New York: Doubleday, pp. 197-200.
   Overview of Bontemps' entire career and discussion of
   the poems in Personals. Bontemps is also briefly mentioned
   under various headings elsewhere in the book.

1976

3   SINGH, AMRITJIT. The Novels of the Harlem Renaissance. Uni-
     versity Park, Pennsylvania: Pennsylvania State University
     Press, 175 pp., passim.
        Treats the common themes of twenty-one novels published
     by Black writers between 1923 and 1933. Bontemps' God Sends
     Sunday is discussed under various headings such as "Race and
     Sex," and Bontemps' account of the period in The Harlem
     Renaissance Remembered is employed extensively as a source.

Indexes

Index — James Weldon Johnson

Index — Arna Wendell Bontemps